S0-BZV-126

RAVE REVIEWS OF THE BOOK AND 20 YEARS OF TEACHING AND TRAINING COACHES

"Coaching is an art form that requires strong, fundamental skills in order to help clients achieve the success they desire. Marion Franklin has done a fine job of capturing these skills in her new book, *The HeART of Laser-Focused Coaching*. **New and experienced coaches alike will benefit greatly from the detailed strategies and wisdom shared from her years of experience.** Marion is a Master Coach with integrity, who clearly has her clients' best interest at heart. You'll have yours, too, when you read *and use* this book!"
~ Cheryl Richardson, *New York Times* bestselling author of *Take Time for Your Life*

"Are you looking for a good resource to ensure great results when you coach? Basic coach training can only take you so far. **Even though I have been coaching for over 20 years, *The HeART of Laser Coaching* gave me new techniques and jogged my memory about practices I had forgotten but were once significant in my client interactions, and business success.** I am grateful for Marion's commitment to document the best of her coach training in one book at that easy to follow and apply. I will keep my copy close by to regularly refresh my skills."
~ Dr. Marcia Reynolds, MCC, past global president of ICF and author of *The Discomfort Zone: How Leaders Turn Difficult Conversations into Breakthroughs.*

"I am honestly blown away by the absolute "usability" of *The HeART of Laser-Focused Coaching!* As a long-time master level coach, **I rarely find any 'how-to' books as meaningful and easy to immediately incorporate into my coaching...with concepts, reminders and actual steps I can take NOW to further my coaching skills.**

i

I so appreciate what Marion has put together in such a readable and usable manner."
~Bobette Reeder, MCC, Past-President, ICF; Co-founder, The Coach Initiative; Co-founder, Conversation Among Masters

"Marion's life and professional experience as a coach and trainer is evident on every page of her book. **Her straightforward and accessible approach makes even the masterful coach sit up and take notes!** As a training director and teacher, I integrated Marion's coaching acumen and students loved it.
After 18 years of coaching, I joined Marion's training and mentoring and was pleasantly surprised to find that I had so much more to learn! **Soon my coaching became almost magical in its effectiveness, and I earned my MCC.** I could not have achieved it without the practical tools and wisdom Marion has in her book. I believe it will become THE book about coaching!"
~ Merci Miglino, MCC

"It will always stay with me how Marion consistently goes for the 'essence' of what the client says. Marion is especially gifted at going deeper and hearing past the unspoken. She ignores nothing and kindly offers straightforward reflections that illuminate blind spots. Her generous guidance and inspiration have proven invaluable to me to earn my PCC and then my MCC."
~ Simona Gherasim, MCC

"The training I had before paled in comparison, so I credit Marion with really teaching me how to coach. She transformed my approach. **What I learned has leap-frogged my coaching skills and confidence going forward.**"
~ Harvette Dixon, ACC

"Since learning more about multiple laser coaching techniques, none taught by any other coach training program I have attended. **I have noticed an undeniable improvement in my coaching. My clients are experiencing deeper connections** with who they

are, how they think and why they may be behaving in certain ways. It is clearly because I am listening differently and formulating my questions from this knowledge."
~ Stew Berman, PCC

"Marion bridges the gap, presenting things in a logical, practical manner while also 'painting the picture' so beautifully. **This book shows us what masterful coaching really looks, feels, and sounds like when all the pieces are put together.**"
~ Nikki Brown, ACC, The Authors Ally

"**My clients noticed the difference in my coaching within the first two weeks.** Most importantly, what I have gained has bolstered my coaching confidence and helps me step out and take this into the world."
~ Randi Buckley, Mentor Coach, Creator of Healthy Boundaries for Kind People, and writer

"One of the biggest things you helped me with was focusing my coaching approach — I was able to get my coaching **sessions pared down to under 40 minutes consistently, resulting in a much more focused and effective session with a faster client shift.** You introduced me to the concept of multiple mini sessions immediately converting the shift to full awareness and action."
~ Edward Macdonald, MCC, Apex Generation Leadership, CEO

"I'm seeing a huge improvement in the effectiveness of my coaching conversations. **Marion showed me how to structure, channel and utilize my intuition and instincts so that my coaching is elevated to a much more effective level.**"
~ Valerie Liberty, ACC

"Marion Franklin is a coach's coach – a master operating at the top of her game. **If you're really serious about wanting to get right to the heart of what coaching is really all about, then this is for you.**"
~ Steve Kaplan, Chief Mindfulness Officer

"I not only learned new approaches, practices, and disciplines, **I was able to combine the many pieces of my new growth to develop a greater awareness and deepening of my coaching presence.**"
~ Jill Linkoff, ACC

"Marion opened my eyes to a new and better way to coach. And to truly be more masterful in the way that I coach."
~ Terry Yoffee, PCC

"I have come to know that I bring the important tools within me — and Marion has taught me how to find them. **Marion taught me that if I coach well, I can coach anyone or any situation; just bring my full presence, my curiosity, and direct communication.** It took me a while to appreciate the simplicity of it."
~ Bea Brennan, ACC

The He*art* of Laser-Focused Coaching

A Revolutionary Approach to Masterful Coaching

Marion Franklin MS, MCC, BCC

Copyright © 2019 Marion Franklin. All rights reserved. No portion of this book may be reproduced mechanically, electronically, or by any other means, including photocopying, without written permission from the author. It is illegal to copy this book, post it to a website, or distribute it by any other means without permission from the author.

Author Contact: LifeCoachingGroup.com

Thomas Noble Books

Wilmington, DE

ISBN: 978-1-945586-22-4

Printed in the United States of America

Author's note: The names and details of the coaching examples provided in this book are composites based on real situations and have been altered when necessary to respect the confidentiality of the coaching relationship or are included with express consent.

This publication is designed to provide accurate and authoritative information regarding the subject matter covered. It is sold with the understanding that the author is not engaged in rendering professional services. The author and publisher disclaim any responsibility or liability resulting from actions advocated or discussed in this book.

DEDICATION

To my children, David and Karen,
who are my ongoing inspiration.

And in tender loving memory of my parents
who provided unconditional love.

TABLE OF CONTENTS

A WORD FROM MARION

The best life is when we leave a trail.
We leave something on this earth bigger than us.
— Viola Davis

I was recovering from a divorce and groping with uncertainty and not knowing who I was. If I'm not a teacher or a wife, then who am I? I signed up for a series of self-development workshops led by a coach starting with "Identity." The final assignment was to rewrite our life story and read it aloud to the group.

Vulnerability had not been my forte, so sharing personal information was a challenge, and to some degree, still is. As I was reading my story, I still remember the exact moment when everything shifted. I spoke about how sad and disappointed I felt that I was "left" after a long-term marriage. And then it occurred to me that "I" was the one who left the marriage by shutting down. It was a defining moment. I went from feeling like a victim, lost, powerless, and alone to feeling a sense of belonging and self-acceptance.

When I discovered that I wasn't the "angel" in my marriage that I thought I was, I was encouraged by my coach to take responsibility for my behavior, thoughts, and actions. When I saw my entire framework and worldview shift from an old programmed paradigm to a new and more immediate one, I realized that coaching was a way I could help others transform their lives. This led me to enroll in coach training, and that was when my life changed forever.

After going through my transformation, in addition to teaching and mentor-coaching for many years, a distinctive style of storytelling and creating exaggerated metaphors emerged. The heart of my approach, which incorporates an understanding of human behavior, shifted from traditional, transactional coaching techniques to a transformational methodology that yielded successful, long-

1

term client results. My dream was to impart all the wisdom and knowledge gained in my almost twenty-five years of coaching into a book that would give you and your clients the benefit of this unique approach.

The Heart of Laser-Focused Coaching was written after I realized that I couldn't be the only coach who at times felt stuck, insecure, or worried about the value I was delivering in a coaching conversation. Once **I discovered some very simple and powerful techniques,** such as the two questions to hold in mind and the twenty-five coaching themes that underlie all coaching conversations, coaching became effortless. The fear of not knowing where to go and not delivering enough value completely disappeared.

With my unique background as a high school teacher, blended with decades of coaching experience including my work with Thomas J. Leonard, the father of professional coaching, *Laser-Focused Coaching* has been designed to not only show you what Laser-Focused Coaching looks, sounds, and feels like, but also *how* **to coach for permanent, life-altering change**.

It has been my honor to mentor coaches from around the world, to present at conferences, and to train hundreds of new and seasoned coaches. In *The HeART of Laser-Focused Coaching*, you'll find my best thinking on how to become an exceptional coach.

Although there is so much you have already learned, we are coaching evolving, ever-changing human beings and that makes the potential for learning unending. It is my sincere hope that the material provided in this book will kindle greater confidence, purpose, and depth on your journey. And that my journey and experience will inspire you to continue yours.

INTRODUCTION

They call me the coach's coach. I've been involved in the coaching profession since its inception in the 90s. After more than two decades of coaching clients (also known as coachees), teaching coaching, mentoring, presenting at coaching events, and serving as an examiner for coaching certification programs, I realized it was time to share what I learned.

Over the years, I've observed well-intentioned, intelligent people enter the coaching profession only to leave it quickly, either because they couldn't attract clients, or they weren't able to maintain long-term coaching relationships. I've listened to thousands of hours of coaching from group and individual mentoring and certification training and have observed the same problems repeatedly, particularly getting seduced by the client's story, failing to get to the root of the problem, and focusing on results. Accordingly, I devised methods to help coaches avoid these common pitfalls so they can confidently provide in-depth coaching.

Laser-Focused Coaching enhances your ability to assist your clients in creating deep and profound changes. This book is *not* about how to market your coaching business, how to design a website, or how to get more clients. Instead, I present unprecedented concepts and information that will help even the most experienced coach gain new insights and ideas that will transform your coaching into something even more far-reaching and powerful.

The skills presented are effective for *every* coach, no matter your experience level or niche. My approach has been dubbed *Universal Coaching* because it's suitable for coaching any human being in any setting.

3

It doesn't matter if you're a graduate of a coaching program, a Master Certified Coach, studied a bit of coaching, use coaching techniques as an HR professional, manager, or leader, or you're self-taught. It doesn't matter what kind of coach you are — life coach, leadership or executive coach, attention deficit disorder coach, health coach, or any of the other types of coaching niches that have sprung up in the last years. If you call yourself a coach or use coaching skills in the workplace, you will benefit from the insights, skills, innovative techniques, and knowledge you'll gain from Laser-Focused Coaching.

The Heart of Laser-Focused Coaching is different because it:

- Offers simple ways to immediately elevate your coaching
- Illustrates *how* to ask powerful questions that change someone's thinking so the transformation is sustainable over the long term
- Explains *how* to make every question powerful without any lists
- Describes *how* to get to the heart of the matter so the client naturally and organically creates forward, sustainable movement
- Provides "how tos" to make your coaching more efficient and effective
- Shares an in-depth understanding of human behavior that helps you quickly identify what's going on
- Presents twenty-five themes that underlie every coaching situation, making coaching and questioning easier and more impactful.
- Outlines the necessary elements for every coaching conversation
- Uncovers strategies and defenses that clients think support what they want but actually work against their desired results
- Gives a literal, easy-to-follow method of creating a deep and permanent change in your client's perspective

I strongly suspect some of the ideas and concepts may contradict what you have learned or are currently doing. Others might seem uniquely intriguing. In any case, my hope is that you consider trying something different, keeping an open mind, and decide whether the concept is worth holding on to and incorporating.

I'm confident that employing even one or two of the principles in this book can immediately elevate your coaching to a new level and your clients will promptly notice enhanced outcomes. The information presented shows you how to consistently separate the client from the situation and how to get to the heart of situations, dilemmas, and challenges efficiently. In turn, your clients will get long-lasting results instead of temporary solutions.

STRUCTURE OF THE BOOK

The material in the book follows an arc just as we do in our coaching: Establishing a foundational mindset, beginning, middle, and end.

Following are the overall elements of a coaching conversation. Laser-Focused Coaching explains each aspect in depth with examples and comparisons to help you master each phase of the conversation.

THE ANATOMY OF A COACHING CONVERSATION			
	THE BEGINNING	THE MIDDLE	THE END
Laser-Focused Mindset	1) Opening question 2) Client story 3) First question *after story* 4) Agreement	5) Discerning truth from perception 6) The shift / change in perspective 7) Looping	8) Optional bonus question 9) Support (resources) 10) Closing and championing

The first part, The Laser-Focused Mindset, sets the stage for objective, unbiased listening, true coaching presence, and letting go of formulas and feeling the need to prove your value. Following this, Parts II, III, and IV are divided into the beginning, middle, and end as outlined. Some of these elements may happen in differing stages or may appear more than once.

Part I: "A New Approach" distinguishes Laser-Focused Coaching from traditional coaching. We'll look at the elements of a typical

Laser-Focused Coaching conversation and then build the foundational structure needed to guide you through the rest of the book. You'll also learn how to go into your client's past while staying out of the realm of therapy and within the ethical boundaries of coaching.

Part II: "The Beginning" details the Laser-Focused mindset, which includes letting go of formulas and models while establishing strong presence and objectivity. I discuss how to listen at a deeper level including data collection and recognizing the triggers that get in the way of good listening. Once the foundation is set, you'll discover the detailed anatomy of a coaching conversation that will help you integrate the elements that belong in a coaching conversation without being formulaic. Also included is an emphasis on the first question *after* the client's story, that often determines the depth of the conversation. You will see that there can be several questions that lead up to the agreement before deepening it.

Part III: "The Middle" explains how to stay out of the client's story and the unimportant details by using the "traffic helicopter approach." I discuss discerning truth from perception and how to increase curiosity so that you're not sucked into taking everything the client says at face value. Included in this section are the *priceless themes that underlie all coaching conversations* and make it easy to quickly identify what's going on underneath the words. You'll discover how to laser in on the heart of the matter and to get to the source of the challenge so you can focus on transforming thinking instead of managing immediate symptoms. You will learn how to get the client to summarize and organically create their own actions.

Parts IV, V, and VI: "The End" includes helping a client follow through and design their own supportive environment. I've also included advanced, masterful coaching techniques as well as challenges faced by coaches at *all* levels. While there is information about the types of clients and their communication styles, I focus primarily on how to make your coaching easier, more effective, and more efficient.

CAVEAT AND INVITATION

Before we begin, I'd like to start with a *caveat* and an *invitation*.

The caveat: What I share is not necessarily the right way, the best way, and it's certainly not the only way. It has evolved from my experience and has proven to be highly effective in transforming lives while serving numerous coaches to become far more effective.

The invitation: Embrace everything as if learning it for the first time. Be open to exploring and learning techniques in a different way, and more importantly, be willing to try new things. Experiment. See what happens. If after experimenting, you find something doesn't work for you, by all means let it go. But I think you'll find that the majority of these time-tested principles and practices are effective. Most importantly, the information is practical, usable, and sustainable for each and every coach.

To help solidify and incorporate the information, I invite you to use a journal so you can record your insights and ideas as you read. You'll also benefit from completing the questions for reflection at the close of each chapter. They are designed to help you deepen your thinking and apply the ideas to your coaching work immediately. Writing down your answers to these questions will help you tap in to your creativity and connect the principles with what you already know — a key component of successful learning. Consider sharing your thoughts with colleagues and, of course, trying things out with your clients.

Our world needs extraordinary coaches! People are longing to grow, to be free from habitual patterns and beliefs that keep them unfulfilled and stuck. People want to reach for a better life than they have today. Regardless of the type of coaching you do, or the setting in which you work, your coaching can and should consistently foster life-changing results. Thank you for choosing this empowering work!

To receive the **Top 10 Myths Coaches Believe**, go to: http://www.lifecoachinggroup.com/readergift

PART I:
A NEW APPROACH

CHAPTER 1

THE FOUNDATION FOR LASER-FOCUSED COACHING

You cannot teach a man anything.
You can only help him discover it within himself.
— Galileo Galilei

BECOMING A MORE MASTERFUL COACH

To differentiate my approach from others that might be more familiar, we first need to understand what Laser-Focused Coaching is and how it differs.

THINGS WE ALREADY KNOW ABOUT COACHING

- Coaching emphasizes experiencing the present moment and shifting perspective and viewpoint. Unlike some types of therapy, it doesn't focus deeply on the past. The emphasis is on what is possible in the present looking toward the future.
- Coaching involves forming a partnership with your client to help them move forward in ways that are authentically satisfying. Satisfaction can come from resolving situations, dilemmas, conflicts, and concerns, and from figuring out how to create, grow, and expand.
- Coaching is about finding a way to change what isn't working or improving on something that is working. It addresses desires, problems, or situations in the present.

- Coaching uses powerful techniques (tools, support, and structure) to help clients clarify and stay focused on their priorities.
- The process of coaching can contribute to creating prosperity, balance, and fulfillment in all areas of life. Through coaching, a client can achieve their vision (what they want in life) by breaking it down into smaller, more manageable steps. Each conversation moves the client closer to what they really want.
- Talking with a friend can be helpful, but coaching offers undistracted listening that is non-judgmental, trusting, honest, and exceptionally objective.
- A coach is a resource with a large tool kit for assisting clients in developing and pursuing their vision, so they achieve positive and permanent results.

The coaching process can be broken down into three simple and easy steps:

1) Identify the ideas, thoughts, or beliefs that keep your client from getting what they want.

2) Help them shift their perspective so that they can feel good about themselves and move forward.

3) Help them capitalize on their strengths to achieve fulfillment and their full potential.

Coaches accomplish this by finding out where their client is now, what their ideal situation is, and how to close the gap between the two.

All coaching has the same focus — to help the client:

- Become more self-aware
- Discover what is keeping them "stuck"
- Create more prosperity, balance, and fulfillment in their life and/or work

But it's how you get there that makes the difference. Now that we have established a baseline, let's look at how Laser-focused Coaching is unique, efficient, and gets to the point deep within.

THE LASER-FOCUSED COACHING APPROACH

In Laser-Focused Coaching, all of the above is true, but there are some major distinctions. The coach *truly* focuses on the client — who the person is, what they think is true, how they behave, and what they value. All of the extraneous details become irrelevant. The coach is able to completely release the need to perform or prove their value. As opposed to focusing on results, the intention is on purposeful exploration leading organically to long-term transformation that affects all areas of a client's life. The client naturally creates their own forward movement from a highly motivated perspective. From the literal first question, more profound, insightful coaching is underway.

A Laser-Focused coach knows how to create and demonstrate a collaborative relationship by providing context for questions and pertinent reflection. It's not about focusing on solving the problematic situation because the solution is actually a by-product. Trying to get to a solution or action plan before exploring the client's thinking, behavior, ideas, and values is the same as asking an inappropriate question such as "How much money do you make?"

Most people think coaching is about helping clients. While we do help them, that is not our aim in Laser-Focused Coaching.

> *Our role is to shine a light on something*
> *our client cannot see for themselves.*

And with that light, clients discover things they couldn't see before, thus helping becomes the by-product.

13

CONVENTIONAL COACHING VERSUS LASER-FOCUSED COACHING

The most common approach to coaching usually follows a learned formula or model to solve a problem. The focus is on action and results, making sure the client takes specific steps before the next session.

Typical coaching starts with accepting at face value what the client shares. Emphasis is frequently placed on agreeing on the outcome the client requests from the beginning, and then working toward that. The coach typically assists the client in designing an action, and then manages accountability.

With this type of coaching, the coach can feel pressure to perform and find solutions to be seen as worthy. Often the coach fails to realize that they are not responsible for any outcome, and consequently gathers more information than is actually needed. This focus on collecting data prevents efficient and more meaningful coaching.

While the client might seem temporarily pleased, neither the coach nor the client realizes how much more could have come from the coaching had the underlying issue been addressed at the root. In addition to taking a specific action to get a specific result, the client could have attained a new vantage point for their situation or challenge that could affect all areas of their life.

By contrast, what I consider *transformational coaching*, or *Laser-Focused Coaching*, relies on understanding the person, not their situation or problem.

A major distinction is that the coach doesn't automatically accept the client's words as *the* truth, because most of what we hear is likely that person's perception of what is true. Learning how to distinguish truth from perception is the foundation of Laser-Focused Coaching. It's about uncovering the misconceptions to reveal the client's own truth rather than what's true for someone else.

Moreover, in Laser-Focused Coaching, questions posed are consistently provocative and challenge the client's thinking while delving into the real meaning of what they're about: their thinking, behavior, ideas, and values.

Laser-Focused coaches zero in on what's most important underneath their client's words without wasting time, but also without overpowering their client. It's based on deep curiosity and respect for the uniqueness of another human being. It's not formulaic, but rather organic and natural. Laser-Focused Coaching is about going deeper, not broader; that is, getting to the bottom line efficiently and effectively.

In the coaching world, the term *laser coaching* is sometimes used to refer to quick coaching with a specified time limit. You might hear a mastermind leader talk about a ten-minute laser-coaching session, and they might even demonstrate by coaching a participant for ten or fifteen minutes.

However, in this book, Laser-Focused Coaching refers to a specific coaching process to quickly identify a greater truth and provide information that can create an immediate change. Although it isn't the aim, often the timeframe is streamlined because the focus is on getting to the underlying truth efficiently.

It provides clarity and a distinct, profound change in perspective. There is a feeling of release or of removing a burden. It's unique because it highlights the way the client is framing their situation with attention on their word choice. Laser-Focused Coaching emphasizes coaching the "who" and separating the "who" from the client's "story" or situation.

A Laser-Focused coach works deep in the trenches with their client to help them change their thinking, patterns, and habits that propel them forward. Coaching is never routine, and your client's life is changed in profound ways. This isn't because *you* have laid out a path for results. It is because you have the skills to listen in a unique way, ask thought-provoking questions that expand their thinking, and discover subconscious ideas that might be preventing progress. You offer a completely neutral, safe environment for them to determine their path in an organic way.

The coach explores with the client until it becomes evident what the person *really* needs. The initial exploration eclipses homing in on the agreement. Because the coaching goes deep, your client naturally creates their own action(s) and is highly motivated to create their own supportive environment to sustain the action(s) they have chosen.

Laser-Focused Coaching allows a client to:

- Move beyond perceived obstacles
- Discover what they *really* want and need (which often is not the initial desire they voiced)
- Realize a new perspective in thinking that is so powerful they can't go back to their original thinking
- Learn the art of surrounding themselves with people who truly support them
- Organically design their own plan for creating their desired experiences and outcomes
- Achieve meaningful, consistent results that are long-lasting and impact other aspects of their life

Now that I've mentioned some distinctions, note the following comparison between two different approaches just in the first few coaching questions.

* * *

Leah came to her coaching session and said, "I feel vulnerable about my situation and it's difficult to share this." She then launched into, "I want to talk about my daughter and the problems she's having on her swim team. I'm not sure if I should have her coached privately by an outside person or have the swim team coach work with her."

Conventional Approach	Laser-Focused Approach
"Thanks for sharing. What would be a good outcome for our conversation?"	"I understand you want to talk about your daughter and the swim team. I'm curious as to what's making you feel vulnerable and having difficulty sharing?"
Leah responds that she wants to make a decision.	Leah responds that she's concerned that her daughter might be in some kind of trouble and may be cut from the team.
"Let's look at some pros and cons to see which coach would be best for your daughter. What are some reasons for getting an outside person?"	"I can understand how worrisome this is. What would that mean for you?"

In the conventional approach, notice that the coach accepted what Leah said at face value, glossed over the opening statement, and dove right into solving the problem. The coach immediately asked for a result. The questions centered on choosing the swim coach and led Leah to action steps to choose the best resource.

This approach is not wrong; it's just not exceptional or life-changing. It deals with Leah's symptoms, which might be temporarily alleviated (choosing the best coach for her daughter), but it does not get to the root of the issue like the Laser-Focused approach (Leah's deeper concerns about her daughter). By choosing to pursue the pros and cons, the coach was focused on their own agenda rather than Leah's agenda by choosing how to begin.

Now, let's look at the same scenario using a Laser-Focused Coaching approach:

The Laser-Focused coach acknowledged what Leah wanted and immediately picked up on and questioned her emotion.

The first question the coach asked was "What's making you feel vulnerable and having difficulty sharing?" Right off the bat, this question didn't ignore *why* Leah shared what she did. Her seemingly offhand comment had to be relevant, and because the opening sentiment wasn't ignored, the coach was able to get to the heart of the matter rather quickly. Notice that the response already revealed significant information.

Then the coach acknowledged Leah's concern and asked a question specifically addressing *her* — not the daughter or the decision. "What's making you feel vulnerable...?" The aim of a Laser-Focused coaching session is to understand the client, explore what is troubling about their situation and ascertain how they would like to feel instead. This helps them discover what thoughts or ideas are in the way of that. In the above scenario, Leah's vulnerability was based on her fear that something was seriously wrong with her child.

A Laser-Focused coach doesn't just accept at face value what their client claims they want from the coaching session. In Leah's case, it might have been that she believed her child's progress was a reflection of her own worth. Perhaps Leah struggled in school and is triggered by painful memories. Or it might have been some other reason entirely. By asking questions and remaining open, we unlock possibilities beyond our limited perception or possible interpretations of what our client is saying. We truly trust them as the expert on themselves and give them the opportunity to discover their own answers by shining the light on their darkness.

As you can surmise, despite some of the common goals of coaching, such as seeing things from a new perspective and moving beyond obstacles, the outcome can be vastly different. Using the Laser-Focused approach, we get sustainable results in less time and with less effort. We address the heart of the problem instead of the symptoms. This allows our client to change their thinking permanently and experience more profound results.

Notice that within only a few questions into the conversation, the results are already completely different. This is just the beginning. Imagine how continuing to use this approach could dramatically change your client's outcome.

This is exactly what I'm going to show you how to do in this book. You'll learn how to:

- Recognize and let go of your own agenda (even if you don't think you have one)
- Discern truth from perception
- Listen more deeply to identify themes, temporary strategies, and patterns that don't support your client
- Ask questions that make your client do all the thinking instead of providing more details and then you having to formulate what to ask next
- Make your questions consistently open and powerful, often through considered reflection and by providing context
- Prevent going in circles and getting lost in the details
- Not worry about what to ask when you feel unsure or stuck
- Gracefully and collaboratively end a conversation

The building blocks are simple, practical, and give the results you (and more importantly your clients) crave in less time. Step-by-step guidelines, examples, and questions for reflection work synergistically, making it easier to learn the techniques. And with consistent practice, you'll embody the material and reach new heights of coaching expertise.

Intrigued? If you're ready to explore how to make your coaching consistently transformational, begin by answering these questions.

QUESTIONS FOR REFLECTION

- What are your current coaching strengths/challenges?
- What are your thoughts about enhancing those strengths with new skills and techniques that might be radically different from what you have learned or have been practicing?
- What are some potential distinctions between what you've been doing and what is possible?

PART II:
THE BEGINNING

CHAPTER 2

THE LASER-FOCUSED MINDSET

*The very best thing you can do for the
whole world is to make the most of yourself.*
— Wallace Wattles

THE ANATOMY OF A COACHING CONVERSATION			
	THE BEGINNING	THE MIDDLE	THE END
Laser-Focused Mindset	1) Opening question 2) Client story 3) First question *after* story 4) Agreement	5) Discerning truth from perception 6) The shift / change in perspective 7) Looping	8) Optional bonus question 9) Support (resources) 10) Closing and championing

Everything begins with the right mindset and it's just as important as the actual coaching. If the coach is distracted or not able to be fully present, it is a disservice to the client. Before delving into the specific elements of a coaching conversation, let's look at some key elements for developing true coaching presence.

BLANK SLATE

If you can imagine a completely objective person without expectations of any kind, you might describe that person as a blank slate — someone free of preconceived ideas about what is coming or what "should" happen. While it's hard to imagine being truly objective without expectations, it is precisely how great coaches approach every coaching conversation. They are

23

flexible, open to whatever shows up, and able to move in whatever direction is needed.

The reason for this mindset is to allow them to be authentic and natural, which in turn releases the inclination to perform or be brilliant in order to be effective.

Trying to be brilliant gets in the way of good listening and creating a true breakthrough for your client.

NOT KNOWING

Picture coming to the conversation not knowing anything and trusting that whatever you need to know will show up. If you have preconceived notions or concerns about how your session will turn out, you will be concerned with doing everything right; that is exactly what detracts from good coaching. It is crucial to not try to be right, smart, or brilliant.

Be willing to be wrong about any attitude or belief. You might ask a question that is totally off base, yet it could allow your client to see the situation clearly. A question that seems off base is not an error. Instead, it shows that you're curious and could even lead to clarity for your client.

Success comes from letting go of the need to provide value or reach a specific outcome.

This comes from practice, experience, and a neutral approach that allows the conversation to flow.

To maintain a Laser-Focused mindset, you must:

- Trust in the process of coaching
- Trust in your client
- Trust in yourself

IT ALL BEGINS WITH YOU

The most important element of Laser-Focused Coaching is you!

One of the foundations of your own transformation as a coach is understanding the mindset, attitudes, and beliefs used by outstanding coaches.

No matter how seasoned or brilliant a coach is, there will still be moments of having no idea where the conversation is going. I still have these moments, and chances are you do too. The difference for experienced coaches is that they know they can trust the process and the idea of *not* knowing isn't uncomfortable.

The key to meaningful coaching is to let go of these moments of not knowing and trust yourself, your client, and the process. While it might seem counterintuitive, part of trusting in the process is about trusting that what you have learned will show up naturally, and that no matter how doubtful you are, it will turn out well.

Some coaches feel like they have "imposter syndrome." They believe they don't provide enough value to make a significant difference or warrant getting paid. You might have experienced such a belief early on and decided you needed to practice more with pro bono clients. Or maybe you have hesitated to state your prices or have spent hours designing your logo and business card instead of connecting with clients.

It's important to know that you bring great value to your client when you listen, ask questions about who they are, and then help them work with that information. You don't have to know more than they do, understand the details of their career, or have the same expertise they possess. An accountant doesn't need a coach to crunch numbers but perhaps for interpersonal skills. Everyone encounters problems that can't be solved on their own. Even the CEO of a global company needs support to see and create new perspectives.

Who you are as a coach is just as important as what you know. A Laser-Focused mindset helps you feel empowered in your ability to provide your clients with consistent transformational coaching experiences. The concepts throughout this chapter and several others will help you learn to trust yourself — no matter what.

YOUR PRESENCE AS A COACH

There are five ways you can become present — through the five senses. If you are truly listening, seeing, smelling, tasting, or touching, you are present.

To be present in a coaching conversation, focus on what you're hearing. As long as you're open, non-judgmental, curious about the person, undistracted, and focused on listening to what is said and what is not said, you are present.

When you speak with your client, it's important to be fully conscious and create a spontaneous relationship. Be open, flexible, and appear confident even when you don't feel that way. Avoid going in with an agenda, thinking you know what to expect, pretending to have the "right" answer, or panicking when you don't know what's going on. Strive to be openly curious, and most importantly, neutral almost to a fault.

As a coach, there will be times in the conversation when your own thoughts will be distracting, confusing, or filled with doubt. Notice those thoughts and return your attention to listening to your client. It's similar to meditation (clearing and redirecting thoughts), but in coaching we come back to listening to the client. As you gain more experience using transformational techniques, those doubts and lack of trust in the process begin to melt away.

If you find yourself becoming anxious because you don't know where the conversation is going, refocus on deep listening and *ask your client what is needed*. For example, you can simply ask, "What would be most helpful at this point?"

Over time you may hear similar client stories and lose focus because you think you know where the conversation is going. However, making these assumptions can get you in trouble because they take away from presence and deeper listening.

Think of it like a movie with a sudden plot twist that takes you by surprise. It's the same when your client is telling a story that is familiar; you have to be prepared for a twist so you can remain connected. Masterful coaching means that at any moment in the conversation you have absolutely, positively no clue where the conversation will end up; you are simply following the client's responses to your questions. It's helpful to imagine that you're listening as if for the first time — as if you have no clue as to what's coming.

LET GO OF THE FORMULAS

Masterful coaching does not have an explicit formula or model. Instead, it's organic in nature as you respond naturally to what your client offers.

While there are particular elements that belong in a coaching conversation, there is no precise formula. After they have shared their initial story, explore the person (not their situation) before homing in on a specific topic for discussion. What your client initially thinks they want often changes when you explore in more depth.

It's important that the conversation is flowing, organic, and natural. Don't use industry jargon; you should never need to explain a word or expression to your client. Use everyday language, just as you would with a friend over lunch.

Contrary to popular belief, put away your list of preplanned coaching questions. Great questions arise from great listening, they don't arise from a list. Simply asking, "What makes that a challenge for you?" or "What would that mean?" can be the most powerful and revealing question of the whole conversation.

27

In taking a transformational approach to coaching, questions arise in the moment based on what you hear. Yet as simple as such natural questions are, they can (and often do) have the most profound impact. You are responding to what your client presents instead of making them respond to what *you* present.

In a masterful coaching session, awareness is created constantly, consistently, and throughout the conversation. It is often described as coming in waves. The client's awareness can come from your:

- Reflection (your interpretation)
- A challenging question
- An observation
- Intuition
- Silence
- Feedback provided by the coach

Notice that none of these techniques require advanced planning, brilliant questions, or cutting-edge thinking. They don't rely on seeking the one big "aha!" moment. This is something many coaches strive for and end up missing important opportunities. Instead, rely on being present, attuning to your client, and following the trail of breadcrumbs they leave for you.

When taking this approach, the "ahas!" come in small, subtle waves that build over the course of the conversation. When you pressure yourself to come up with questions to get an "aha!" you're focusing on yourself instead of the client. Feeding your ego then takes precedence over the client's results, and you become unable to listen deeply to get to the heart of the matter. When you put your client first and focus your full attention on them, somehow the answers reveal themselves and the way forward becomes clear.

BE FRIENDLY, NOT FRIENDS

As a coach, you are a professional, objective outsider with permission to be direct. On the other hand, a friend has a vested interest in maintaining the relationship permanently and can share personal information freely.

So how do you stay friendly and not become a friend? Focus the conversation on your client, not on you. When you do this well, you don't get sucked into their emotions or the details about their situation. In general, don't bring your experiences or opinions into the conversation unless they're based on something your client shared, no matter how tempting it might be. However, if you feel compelled to share something you have experienced or done, you don't necessarily have to reference yourself.

It's important to remain professional with your client. Avoid looking to them to fulfill your personal needs, such as the need to socialize, to be liked, to be praised, etc. Refrain from agreeing with them or comparing yourself to their situation, as this can get in the way of your role as the objective listener. Even if you strongly identify with them or have had a similar experience, use what you learned from your situation to question them without mentioning how you learned it. *Friendly* means staying objective and enjoying your client. It doesn't mean sharing and commiserating the way friends do.

In a professional, friendly relationship, you stimulate progress. It's much more than a chat. You're helping your client deepen their self-awareness and move forward.

BE YOUR OWN COACH FIRST

One of the most important aspects of becoming truly masterful is to work on your own problems. That doesn't necessarily mean solving them completely; it means continually working on your personal development and growth. The more a coach works on themselves, the better their coaching.

It's uncanny how the things you work on show up with your clients. Not only is it important to learn from your clients, but it's also beneficial to use your clients' challenges as a springboard for working on areas *you* need to focus on. For instance, if your client is challenged by boundaries, it's an opportunity to look at your own boundaries and note where some work might be needed. As you know, it's easier to help someone else than it is to help ourselves. Having your own coach not only helps to reveal blind spots, but I've consistently noticed that my coaching improves just by receiving coaching.

YOUR EGO AND THE USE OF "I"

It's important to keep the word *I* out of the coaching conversation as much as possible. Your client doesn't need your advice or to hear about something that worked for you. They need to know what will work for them because everyone is different, and they certainly aren't you, are they?

Moreover, your client is *always* right. Let go of your ego and let them be right. For example, your client states, "The grass is purple." Instead of contradicting them, ask the question "What has you coming to that conclusion?" In other words, don't make them wrong or set up barriers. Let them explain their conclusion. When you do this, you gain trust. Letting them explain doesn't mean you agree with them; it means you respect their different point of view. Give them the space to explore their ideas so that you get closer to the root of their beliefs and stories. This is where true transformation can occur.

The following is a paraphrased quote about coaching from Rachel Naomi Remen, who wrote *Kitchen Table Wisdom* and is a leader in integrative medicine:

> Our work as coaches is to be of service. If we try to help or fix them, we are making a judgment that the person is broken. Helping and fixing lead only in one direction; they are draining, and they keep us from serving the dream in other people. They imply that we don't trust the person's potential and that we have more expertise. A good message for your clients is "Your life matters." We want them to understand that who we are is as important as what we do.

The coach's focus is to be of service and to serve clients from our soul and not from our ego; it is not to fix or solve their problems. Once a coach starts trying to fix or solve a problem, or give advice, they are consulting, not coaching.

When you're able to use these ideas to approach coaching conversations with presence, an open mind, and a commitment to remaining neutral, your clients flourish. They feel more comfortable exploring their deeply held beliefs and perceptions because they know you won't judge them or force them into anything. Few people have the experience of this kind of acceptance. It creates deep trust and a willingness to move out of familiar patterns. That's when transformation can begin!

QUESTIONS FOR REFLECTION

- If you use a coaching formula or model, what might happen if you experiment with letting it go?
- What comes to mind when you read about maintaining presence during coaching and truly trusting yourself, your client, and the process?
- What is different for you (and your client) when you know you are truly present?
- What benefits could consistent transformational coaching have for your current clients?

CHAPTER 3

LISTENING WITH A NEW INTENT

*Most people do not listen with the intent to learn
and understand. They listen with the intent to reply.
They are either speaking or preparing to speak.*
— Stephen Covey

The most significant coaching skill is your ability to listen. People often assume listening is easy since it's one of our senses and we do it all day long. However, a masterful coach learns to listen in a deeper way for the client's truth. It's taken me countless years to master the art of listening, and my hope is that this chapter will instill what I've learned and mastered over time into your everyday practice so you can give your clients a phenomenal coaching experience.

In this chapter, you'll discover some opportunities to collect data about your client from the initial session onward. I also go into detail about the two most important questions to hold in mind during *any* conversation.

WHAT GETS IN THE WAY OF DEEP LISTENING?

No matter who we're listening to (as a coach, friend, parent, etc.), our minds take us away from pure listening. It's natural to fill in the blanks, or have ideas that are not relevant or true, all while someone is talking. Unless someone is really entertaining, it's hard for us to stay focused because everything we hear triggers a reaction or is a clue to something, and then our minds go off on tangents.

When you're not really listening:

- You might miss important information.
- You can lose patience and want to jump right to a solution.
- You could feel embarrassed that you haven't really been listening deeply and want to say something you think is brilliant to prove that you've been paying attention after all.
- You could get distracted and go off on a tangent.

There are signs when you stop listening in a coaching session. Your mind goes off somewhere, you lose focus, or perhaps you feel bored. Deep down you worry that your client will notice or that the session won't have a positive result. And that concern leads to wanting to add value and find a solution which is exactly what keeps the coaching from being masterful.

Let's say Suzanne comes to the session complaining bitterly about her mother. She says her mother calls her every morning, during the workday, and every evening. She laments that she really wants her mother to stop calling so often. Many coaches will start to think things like:

- Does she want to work on this, or she is just venting?
- Where did this come from?
- How does this fit with what we talked about last week?
- Oh, gosh, my mom does the same thing! It's so annoying.

All of these thoughts drive your attention away from Suzanne and make it difficult to listen deeply. You are human, and your mind *will* wander from time to time. What is important is that you learn to notice your wandering thoughts, stop them, and then refocus your attention back to listening.

In Laser-Focused Coaching, we want to do more with our listening. The following concepts help to get underneath the spoken word and hear what is behind their word choices.

COLLECT DATA

From the moment you connect with someone (phone, email, text, or in person), every exchange between you provides data. The definition of *data* is information without any editorial or opinion. Nothing is to be excused or dismissed. All this information is to be stored in your mental "databank" to be retrieved at any time. Even a person's approach and communication style are data.

Ascertaining data in your initial contact is extremely helpful over time. Think about your first impressions when meeting someone new. Suppose someone rubs you the wrong way; you've already "banked" a judgment or opinion about them. In coaching especially, you want to take the data and remain completely neutral and detached; it's just information to be stored.

Let's say Louise, a potential client, contacts you through email. She asks you to call her but doesn't provide a phone number. The omission could be immediately stored as "careless," "overwhelmed," or "anxious," but it could have simply been an oversight. That initial data should be simply information with no interpretation. But when Louise becomes a client, and another situation reminds you of this one, you can now go deeper into determining whether or not there is a pattern.

Suppose Richard, another potential client, contacts you by telephone. He introduces himself, and then before you have a chance to set up an appointment to speak with him, he is talking nonstop about his frustration at work. When he finally takes a breath, he starts asking all sorts of questions about coaching, how much it costs, etc. Pay attention — you're already collecting important data. Without getting hooked or making any judgment, once the relationship is underway you can address this when/if you hear him launching into details before you've had a chance to ask what he wants to focus on for the session. The first time you hear a client imply they have given up what they want for the sake of some else's happiness, it's data. But when you hear it again or there is evidence as they continue, it becomes data in context that can be questioned.

As you work with your clients over time, you'll collect more data. It may be a challenge to accept data as simply information — neither positive nor negative. Yet, to maintain neutrality and foster transformation, it's important to accept anything you learn about your client as simply data and recall it when it's relevant. Otherwise it's too easy to get hooked into their pattern and/or lose objectivity.

EXPLORE OFFHAND COMMENTS

This topic falls under the umbrella of collecting data.

When your client makes an offhand comment, it shouldn't be ignored. Question it, and if they say it's not important, you can move on. However, it would not be okay to totally dismiss it because people bring things up for a reason. Perhaps it's just something they want to get off their chest or it could be something disturbing them, impacting the other topic they want to discuss.

A client might say, "I'm having a really horrible time with my boss today, but I want to talk about my situation with my mother." It would behoove you to ask a question about the boss situation despite their being dismissive about it. This is a perfect opportunity to ask yourself one of the two critical questions: "Why are they telling me this?" Pay attention to offhand comments as they often mean something.

Consider this example based on a group mentor call:

* * *

Ben, a VP, recently hired a coach. At the coaching session he said, "I don't often ask for help. Here's my situation. I'm having problems with one of my direct reports (a director). He doesn't seem to understand instructions, and I'm finding that I have to follow up far more than is appropriate. I feel like I'm wasting so much valuable time making sure he completes things and does them correctly. At this point, my frustration level is boiling over."

Ben's first coach unfortunately missed an opportunity to key in on something important. There was a reason Ben mentioned that he doesn't often ask for help.

> **There's a reason behind EVERYTHING a client shares in a coaching session.**

The coach could have asked a question to help Ben explore why he doesn't often ask for help; instead she asked about his frustration with the director.

The second coach started over and said, "I can hear how frustrating this must be with your director, and I also heard that you don't often ask for help. What is that about?" Ben responded, "I don't want to be seen as a bad guy, and I'm not convinced that these are problems that need to be talked about." The coach then asked, "What might be the connection between not wanting to be seen as a bad guy and the situation with your director?" Ben replied, "I've always been told that I should keep the peace and not rock the boat." The conversation continued until Ben realized that this old message wasn't serving him in all situations.

The offhand "by the way" comment (I don't often ask for help) was the heart of the problem, and this is frequently the case.

MAINTAIN NEUTRALITY

Maintaining neutrality is perhaps the most difficult, but also one of the most important aspects, and it's at the core of being a true professional.

Where is the line between authentic response and neutrality? The key is that whatever you share and whatever you question cannot have a "charge," meaning it should have no emotion or opinion behind it. Instead of putting a positive or negative spin on what you share, see your sharing as simply a point to be made.

It's especially important to remain neutral when sharing your observations, feedback, and ideas. For example, let's say your client has been talking for quite a long time without pause. Instead of trying to make them see that their behavior is impacting you, or sharing your frustration (even unconsciously, such as in the emotion behind your words), you might say something like "I've been listening to you for a long time now, and there is so much detail it's really hard to stay focused. What do you think when you hear this?" This approach allows you to just share what you noticed and then give the choice of response to your client. It presents factual, objective information — the *data* — and allows them to decide where to go next. It's not that you can't feel anything or need to shut yourself down — it's about not getting dragged into their emotion or situation to the extent that you can't stay objective and helpful.

You don't know what your client is going to say even if you use a preparation form. You can't prepare for how they'll respond to a question or what might trigger them. You might have an initial opinion or judgment, such as "This is a frail person who needs a lot of hand-holding," but instead the person tells you a story about how they were really empowered. The bottom line is that if you don't stay open, neutral, and objective, you'll likely get caught up in their story and miss what's essential for their transformation.

How do you balance all the data you've gathered about your client and still show up completely neutral? Approach each coaching conversation as a fresh blank slate. If needed, you can go back to your databank and ask a question about something you observed over time or heard in a prior conversation, but only if that seems appropriate in the moment. The data is stored in your mind — everything about your client from the first moment of contact: the types of questions they ask; their style of communication; their ideas, beliefs, patterns, progress, or lack of progress — *everything* is stored to use in the future when appropriate and needed. For example, you might recall something stated in a prior conversation that seems to contradict what they're saying now. (You may find it helpful to write things down but keep in mind that anything in writing could be subpoenaed in a court of law.)

HOLD IN MIND TWO CRITICAL QUESTIONS

If you always hold these two critical questions in your mind when listening to *anyone*, especially a client, it automatically deepens your listening and your curiosity:

1) **Why are they telling me this?**

2) **What's making this a problem for *this* person?**

These questions should not be articulated out loud. They are designed to help you be more curious about the person, sustain your focus, and really listen to *understand what the underlying problem or "faulty thinking" is for your client*. They will help you:

- Focus on your client, not the story being shared
- Recognize their emotional state while learning how they think and process information
- Stay curious without being nosey about the details
- Listen for what is not being said or what is underneath the words
- Discover opportunities to ask questions that expand your client's thinking

Here are some brief examples of how holding these questions in mind help to figure out what the client needs.

* * *

Jerry told an involved story about an argument between two of his co-workers during a staff meeting. He spoke about the intensity between the two of them and how each one would not back down on their point of view. He mentioned that when people tried to intervene, they ignored them and kept arguing.

His coach asked lots of questions about the people who were arguing, their dispute, and other details of the event. She got lost in the particulars of the story and the session spiraled to a discussion about the people arguing.

Imagine if the coach was curious and wondered why Jerry was so invested in an argument that didn't involve him? What was his point in going into so much detail? Thinking about "Why is he telling me this?" and "What is making this a problem for him?" could have led to questions to help Jerry explore the feelings, threats, or issues the argument created for him.

* * *

Patricia was hoping to go on a medical mission. In fact, it had been her long-term dream. She said, "I've been counting on funds from a real estate deal to provide the financing. However, after all of the unexpected transaction fees, I received only about ten percent of what I had calculated. I'm so devastated, and I think I have to give up on my dream."

The coach said, "It sounds like very deep disappointment and seems like a person who put all of their eggs in one basket. What comes up hearing that?"

Patricia was silent for quite some time before saying, "You are right and hearing that, I realize I didn't plan well at all for something so important to me." By the end of the conversation, Patricia felt empowered and altered her negative, limited trajectory, and planned to consult with her CPA and get creative accounting advice. (Soon after, she was able to cobble the funds together to fulfill her dream.)

The first question exemplifies listening for *why* she is telling me this (her deep disappointment) and what's making it a problem for her (didn't plan any options). To this day, she reminds me how the question literally changed her life.

If I had asked, "What will it mean for you to give up your dream?" it may have led to a downward spiral because I was buying into the story that Patricia messed up and can't do what she really wants.

Instead, I empathized but also named the crux of the problem and questioned it.

I will be exploring these two critical questions at length in Chapter 4.

SPEAK THEIR LANGUAGE

In coach training, you often hear that it's beneficial to use the client's language. However, there are instances in which this can feel uncomfortable or strange. Even though that may be the case, it's helpful for the client to use their vocabulary so they don't have to interpret what you're saying or asking. For example, if they use the word *photograph* and your word is *picture*, use their word. If they use the expression "out of pocket," and your tendency is to substitute "unavailable," hold in your mind that you're partnering with your client and that it is most effective to use their language even if it feels unnatural. This also helps your client feel heard and understood.

ELIMINATE JARGON — IT ISN'T UNIVERSAL

My overall rule of thumb is that I should never have to explain a word or expression to a client. I think to myself, "Would you say this word or expression to a friend over lunch?" Coaching is supposed to sound like an everyday conversation with the exceptions of the 80/20 dialogue rule and the sharing of personal information. (The 80/20 rule is a guideline that you speak about 20 percent of the time and allow the client to speak 80 percent of the time.) Often, I hear coaches use words or expressions that have to be explained, such as:

- "What do you have to lean in to?" instead of "What could be the opportunity?"
- "Who do you have to be?" instead of "What are some characteristics you would like to see in yourself?"
- "How do you need to show up?" instead of "What do you need to do to prepare for the conversation?" or "What do you want people to notice about you?"

Although coaches often use the word *belief*, it's ironic that it can have a negative connotation. It is distinctly coaching terminology. If you say to your client, "I hear this belief that you always have to go above and beyond," the client could potentially hear, "How could you really think that's okay?" I much prefer the word *thought* or *idea,* as they seem more natural and non-judgmental. For example:

"I heard the thought that…." However, for purposes of discussing the client's ideas and thoughts, I will default to the word *belief* because you are familiar with that terminology.

USE SILENCE REGULARLY

> *A smart person knows how to talk.*
> *A wise person knows when to be silent.*
> — Roy T. Bennett

Silence is one of the most important tools in the coaching tool kit and the one least effectively used. It means not only being silent after you ask your question, but also staying silent after your client initially answers your question.

Coaches do not leave enough silence! When a coach asks a question, and their client answers, the coach often follows with another question because they believe the client is finished speaking. But some people need time to process the question. Others speak as they are thinking, and it's up to the coach to listen to their "thinking" and realize there is more coming. The client might just be taking a pause in their thinking and their wheels are still turning. A masterful coach should be able to decipher the fact that thinking is still going on despite hearing a preliminary response, and the client still needs even more thinking time. It's better to err on the side of caution and stay quiet.

The only time it's okay to ask another question right after your client responds is when you simply asked for information rather than stimulated the client to think, as with a question like, "What day did that happen?"

Especially for new coaches, silence can be exceptionally uncomfortable and feel as though you've said something wrong or you've lost the client. However, as uncomfortable as it might be, it distinguishes elementary coaching from masterful coaching.

> *Wait for the client to speak first no matter how difficult or uncomfortable it is to stay quiet.*

This is *especially* true after a question that makes your client think, because they may not be finished answering even though they have replied. Allow even more time in this case, even though they *seem* to be finished. Here's an example:

Coach: What did that comment mean for you?

Client: Hmm, I hadn't thought about what it meant. [The *Hmm* or if there's silence before responding is a clue to stay quiet even longer.] I guess it means that she's waiting for me to address the issue first. [*Allow silence again.*] Although as I think about it, I'm not sure that is my place. After all…."

The last thing you want to do is disrupt your client's thinking. It's like having a fabulous dream and the alarm goes off; it immediately interrupts the dream and there is no going back. If your client thinks there's too much silence, they'll let you know.

Silence is especially necessary after your client answers a provocative question. Just wait; they might be emotional or most likely still thinking even after giving an initial response. They may need a lot of space before being asked another question.

Question/answer/question/answer can be a sign of ineffectual coaching. When I demonstrate coaching, people immediately notice how much silence I allow because people have a need to fill in the silence. Therefore, if you just stay quiet, your client will be happy to fill in the space with important data.

Another time when silence is often not used effectively is when a coach asks a question and the client doesn't respond. The tendency is to immediately rephrase the question instead of staying quiet and realizing that they need more time before responding.

Even after your client responds "I don't know…" after a thinking question, it's still advisable to stay quiet and see if that simply means they don't want to answer, are afraid to answer, or really need to think about the answer. In any event, silence is appropriate because almost every time there's a further response.

For example, a coach asks a client, "What are you afraid of?" and the client answers, "That I will never be okay." If the coach asks *any* question right after that, it creates a disconnect because the client's response was particularly deep. If the client answers, "I don't know," it's possible they don't. But more often than not, they *do* know but may not want to say it aloud or they need time to think and digest their thoughts. Your client may require an enormous amount of space to think and digest. *Any* question would take them out of that space and bring them back into their mind. In this instance it's crucial to wait for the client to speak first.

BE EMPATHETIC

While evaluating coaching sessions, I overheard the following interchange:

Client: I'm totally freaked out! I just found out that my husband cheated on me and I don't know what I'm going to do. I don't know if I should tell my children what's going on, and I don't know if this means I'm going to get divorced!

Then I heard the coach parrot: I hear that you're really upset that you just found out that your husband is

44

cheating on you and you're not sure if you should tell the children and you're not sure what this is going to mean for you. Did I get that right?

This response lacks empathy and demonstrates that the coach heard what was said but wasn't truly listening and understanding the client and her feelings. I often hear a coach repeat or even reflect a sentiment as though they're reporting on the weather conditions! Your voice, tone, and pace *matter*. Especially when emotion is evident, it's crucial to let the client know that you empathize and understand the reason for the emotion by "normalizing" their feelings.

Empathy is simple but not easy for many people. The tendency is to try to fix other people's emotions instead of just reflecting their experience back to them. To empathize, identify one or two primary emotions and reflect that information. In the prior example, the client provided the emotion: freaked out, and she shared ways she feels uncertain about her future. An appropriate empathy statement could be, "I get how all of this is freaking you out and that it's a lot of uncertainty to deal with all at once." By putting yourself in their shoes, it's easier to convey the emotion.

Imagine the scenario above if the coach went directly to, "What outcome do you want from this conversation?" This is an example of a "naked," nonresponsive question that is completely inappropriate. It not only ignores what the client said and the feeling behind her words, but also asks her to define an outcome while she's in an emotional state.

A masterful empathic response might be: "It sounds as though you've been blindsided and are understandably upset. What would be helpful in our conversation?" The empathy demonstrates that you understand and when you ask the follow-up question, it is an invitation for them to choose what they want. In this type of situation, instead of "fixing" the client or going into problem-solving, consider that the client may not want anything other than an opportunity to vent and will feel as though they have permission to do so.

CREATE A SAFE AND TRUSTING SPACE

Clients reveal more information when they feel a sense of trust and safety. If they have any doubt or hesitation, they will likely hold back. It is the role of the coach to create a safe space and a trusting environment. Once that is established, the real conversation is underway.

To accomplish this safe and trusting environment, *keep in mind that the relationship is more important than the results.* Yes, results are important, but working with human beings with complex thoughts, feelings, and experiences has to be uppermost in our minds. With a focus on the relationship and letting go of a strong need for results, deeper trust is created, more can be revealed, and clients go far beyond their initial intention. These are the engagements that are sustainable over a longer period of time.

* * *

Erica initially came for coaching because she was unhappy in her job. During our coaching engagement, not only did she change jobs twice, she eventually opened up her own studio. She went from dating to marriage to starting a family. The relationship deepened over a period of several years and went far beyond her initial reason for coaching.

* * *

Melissa came to the call sounding quite upset and immediately shared that she was unexpectedly pregnant. She said she hadn't told her husband or parents yet but had to tell someone. All I did was stay present and let her know I was there. She didn't come for any result as much as wanting to process and be heard. Without many words from me, she said she felt my empathy and connection. Several months later, she shared that because of our coaching relationship, she knew she could trust me to hold the space for her.

Sometimes, coaching is only about the relationship and respecting the client's humanity.

PLAY DUMB TO BE SMART

Your attitude as a coach is critical. If you approach coaching as though you're the expert and you know what's best for your client, not only are you not being a coach, but you're also dismissing your client's wisdom. In fact, the more you can demonstrate curiosity and your desire to understand who your client is, the better your coaching will be.

It is imperative to be willing to be wrong about any attitude or belief. Phrases such as "I'm a little confused" or "I may be wrong, but it seems as though..." not only invite your client to share better information but also demonstrate that you are the outside, objective listener that you should be.

If you put something out there and you're wrong, so what? As long as you get new data, that's what is important. Coaching is not about being right or wrong; it's about getting to the truth for your client. In fact, if you say or guess incorrectly when sharing something, they're happy to share the accurate information. It can actually spur them to share more.

AFFIRM VERSUS ACKNOWLEDGE

As coaches, one of our roles is to support and champion our clients. This is not to be confused with cheerleading. To properly acknowledge our client, providing some context is helpful. When doing so, we're affirming and not just acknowledging. For example:

Acknowledging: "Thanks for sharing that information."

Affirming: "Thanks for sharing that information because it helps me better understand your mindset."

The distinction is that, when affirming, we are being specific and providing context.

It's not appropriate to affirm on a continual basis. However, doing so from time to time makes a difference, because the client feels validated.

* * *

Josh, a client who was dating a lot, told me a story about a woman who called about going out again, and I noticed a change in how he responded. I said, "What I'm really hearing is that the way you handled this particular conversation is so different from how you would've handled it six months ago. It's just showing how much progress you've made and how far you've come. What do you think about that?" Josh replied, "Wow, this is getting easier for me. I didn't realize I was improving. That's so cool." He was appreciative of my noting that he had made progress.

DISTINGUISH: TELLING VERSUS DISCOVERING

When is it appropriate to tell your client something you know versus letting them figure it out for themselves?

When *emotion* is involved, it's best for your client to discover. When they discover the answer for themselves, it has more meaning, more value, and leads to a permanent change. And if the discovery is about them and who they are, only they know the answer.

When it's a fact, a greater truth, or a direct observation, *tell* it. By "a greater truth" I mean something universally accepted as true by most people but not a fact. In these situations, don't frustrate your client by asking them questions to force a discovery. Instead, say what you know and question how they receive it by asking something like "What do you think?"

Here are some examples of greater truths:

- It's harder to find a job during an economic downturn.
- Women talk with friends to create bonds.

- Men identify strongly with their jobs/careers/work.
- Some people are content with the status quo and have no interest in changing.
- People have a tendency to confuse selfish with self-care.

What are some others you can think of that could help to create awareness?

All of the points discussed in this chapter establish a strong foundation for masterful listening. Those that are not new to you bear repeating. Others, such as the two critical questions to hold in mind, will likely contribute to far deeper listening going forward. Becoming more aware of offhand comments contributes further to mastery, but my favorite principle in this chapter is the use of silence — so easy and yet so hard.

QUESTIONS FOR REFLECTION

- What benefits might there be if you were to keep the two critical questions at the top of your mind?
- What has been your experience with silence and how might it change going forward?
- What impact will exploring offhand comments have on your coaching?

CHAPTER 4

SETTING THE FOUNDATION

When you hand good people possibility, they do great things.
— Biz Stone

Now that you have the foundational mindset for Laser-Focused Coaching, the following chapters discuss each component of a coaching conversation in greater detail.

In masterful coaching, no model or formula should be detected. However, every masterful coaching conversation, no matter how short, contains three key elements to move the conversation forward: the beginning, middle, and end. Each element contributes to the deepening partnership between coach and client and helps to create a more meaningful conversation.

- The beginning is for establishing rapport and trust, so the client feels comfortable to share freely.
- The middle is for helping them become aware of where and why they're stuck, or why their thinking is "faulty" so they can gain more awareness about themselves and their situation.
- The end is for putting what's been learned into action, setting up support, and closing down collaboratively.

First, let's examine each element of the beginning segment more closely.

Part II: The Beginning

	THE ANATOMY OF A COACHING CONVERSATION		
Laser-Focused Mindset	THE BEGINNING	THE MIDDLE	THE END
	1) Opening question 2) Client story 3) First question *after* story 4) Agreement	5) Discerning truth from perception 6) The shift / change in perspective 7) Looping	8) Optional bonus question 9) Support (resources) 10) Closing and championing

THE OPENING QUESTION

The very first question a coach asks their client when starting the conversation should immediately imply that this is a professional conversation with a purpose.

Since coaches should not have an agenda, refrain from asking your client for an update at the start. Suppose your last conversation centered around his search for a new job. But in this conversation, the client is in deep distress after finding out he has a serious medical condition. Chances are he will want to talk about his medical condition and not his job search. Therefore, allow him to first share what he wants to discuss, and if appropriate, ask at another point in the conversation for an update on the job search issue. Besides, a client's initial story often includes an update, or it becomes evident during the conversation.

Clients have a tendency to share every detail that comes to mind. If your opening questions are, "What do you want to talk about?" or "How has your week been?" you are effectively inviting a detailed story that can easily move the interaction from a professional coaching conversation to idle chit-chat that lacks focus and intent.

Here's an example of a strong opening question:

"In our time together, what can we focus on that will [bring you value / be of importance / make a difference]?" If they respond, "I don't know," keep in mind that this response basically means they don't have a "story of the week," are hesitant to bring up what is really going on for them, or lack something specific that stands out for discussion. You then have options:

52

- You can ask them to remember why they came for coaching in the first place.
- You can ask what progress they have made since the beginning of the engagement and what still needs to change.
- You can say that there have to be aspects of their life that aren't exactly as they would like, and then ask what would make sense to discuss.

Whether or not the client has a specified topic ready, many of their overall patterns and behaviors are still present. This means that there is always something to explore.

THE CLIENT STORY

Your client typically launches into their story following your tactful opening question. They likely provide details and/or a clear example, as well as something they want to work on. It can go on for quite some time, but listening from your helicopter view, you should be able to synthesize it into something strictly about your client.

Separate the story from who the person is and how they think or behave.

In each example below, note what part belongs to the story, and how the follow-up question is about the person.

- **The story:** My boss told me in private that he is leaving the company, and I want to tell my teammates even though I know it's wrong.

  The person: What is making it hard for you to stay quiet about this?

- **The story:** I want to clean up the clutter in my office.

  The person: What's makes clutter a problem for you? or What makes it important to address at this time?

- **The story:** I need to make a decision as to whether to stay in this department or move to a different one in the company.

  The person: What makes it a difficult decision? or What would help you know what to do?

- **The story:** I'm getting frustrated with my boyfriend who is always late and often backs out of things at the last minute.

  The person: What's making this a problem for you? or What's allowing you to accept this behavior?

We want to avoid questioning the story because that leads us down a rabbit hole that goes in circles, and we won't get new information that helps us get to the client's truth. The object of your questions is to keep the conversation moving forward by getting a better understanding of what's really going on with the person.

THE FIRST QUESTION *AFTER* THE CLIENT'S STORY

> *The first question you ask after the client's initial story can be the most important question of the entire conversation.*

It often determines the depth of the conversation. Your exploration process should always supersede your desire to arrive at a solution. It's an extreme exception that a client knows from the start exactly what the problem is and what they want as a result. What they share is often an example or a concept with something much deeper underneath it.

It's important to keep in mind that *reflection* — that is, "reflecting" your interpretation of the client's information back to them, particularly after their opening story — is critical. They just shared information and want to feel heard and understood.

To build trust and rapport, the first step should be to reflect in your own words what your client said, followed by a short, open, and broad question. Reflection is *not* parroting, but rather includes an interpretation on your part. (More on reflection in Chapter 5.)

Rather than checking your client's story by asking a closed question that they can answer with a yes or no, it's prudent to move right into an open question. Your first question should lead away from the story and toward understanding the person, thereby deepening the conversation immediately.

More often than not, some of the weaker first questions I hear from newer coaches are:

"What do you want as an outcome of this conversation?"

This question does not help build rapport, and the answer usually becomes moot during the conversation. This early on, it's unlikely you will get to the underlying reason or purpose for the client sharing their situation.

If possible, avoid:

"I hear that your boss is giving you a hard time
and you need to figure out if you want to
stay in this job. Did I get that right?"

Asking this "yes or no" question makes it seem as though the coach doesn't know what to ask and/or needs to confirm hearing every word. It's a closed question, which means the coach now has to do the thinking instead of the client. It also appears to be more about the coach proving that they listened well.

"Tell me more about the relationship with your boss."

This question will likely invite more about the story rather than help you understand more about the person. It's not about the relationship, but rather what's behind the fact that there is contemplation of leaving and why it's bothersome for your client.

Instead, consider:

> "It seems as though you are contemplating leaving based on your relationship with your boss. What might be helpful in making this decision?"

or

> "What's important about addressing the prospect of leaving at this time?"

These questions are about the client, move the conversation forward, and will provide useful data to explore what's underneath the problem.

If your client shares something extremely vague, it can be helpful to ask for an example so you can get a better understanding of what they're saying. Or, you could simply ask, "What would be helpful in this conversation?" If at any point you're not 100 percent clear about what they mean, it's crucial that you ask for clarification; however, in doing so, it's prudent to begin with, "Just for clarification…." If you don't fully understand them, the coaching cannot move forward because the focus is cloudy.

Sometimes your client will only provide a concept such as, "I'm having trouble making decisions." Asking for an example might yield data that implies it's not really about decision-making at all but rather a fear of sharing a decision they already made.

As you continue to move into the conversation, remember the two questions you should always be asking yourself when listening to your client:

1) Why are they telling me this?

This question (never to be articulated) helps you listen more acutely to your client, separate the details from the person, and continue to be curious about what motivated them to choose what they shared.

2) What's making this a problem for this person?

Not every person presents a similar response to a challenge. It's your job to understand why *this particular person* has *this particular challenge* when someone else wouldn't have it.

If your client wants to make a decision, it's important to first understand: what's behind making the decision, why now, and what is making it a difficult decision for them? Masterful coaching moves along layer by layer, piece by piece, in partnership with the client. It's not about listing the pros and cons of the decision they need to make; they have likely already done that. It's about exploring and understanding your client, their motives, their thinking, and their behavior. Gathering more details about the decision or their situation isn't helpful in understanding the deeper considerations of motive, thought processes, and behavior.

* * *

Scott begins his coaching session saying, "My aunt and uncle passed away about a year ago and I inherited their house. I've noticed lately that I used to always be punctual. Lately I find myself always late, and it's really bothering me. I'm hoping in this conversation we can look at time management and how I can get back to being on time."

Two seemingly unrelated topics are mentioned. (*Why is he telling me this?*) You don't want to ignore what your client is asking for — better time management — even though it may end up not being relevant as the conversation unfolds. Therefore, address both topics; "I understand that you want to look at time management and this new pattern of being late, and I'm wondering — what does it mean for you to have inherited this house?"

Be careful of diving too deep too fast. Initially if the question was "What do you suppose could be the relationship between the house and the lateness?" it probably would have been too big a question. Scott wouldn't even have thought about any connection.

Not only would you be introducing that concept but also making an assumption and asking for more than Scott might be capable of answering so early in the conversation.

In our coach training class, as Scott continued talking, we discovered that he was upset he was given a house he didn't want. Knowing that being late is often tied to anger or resentment, the coach's question helped to reveal that he didn't really want the house because it ended up taking a huge amount of his energy. Scott saw that his lateness wasn't about time management but was caused by his continual frustration, anger, and resentment. He was then able to *choose* to be punctual again.

SUPPORT THE CLIENT'S AGENDA, NOT YOUR OWN

Coaches often inadvertently set the agenda, particularly when their client offers more than one possibility.

For example, when the client says, "I would like to discuss my father. I also want to talk about my job," and the coach asks, "What is it about your father you want to talk about?" The coach has *made a choice* for the client instead of allowing the client to choose the path they want to take.

A coach can also set the agenda by asking a leading question or making a request. A leading question seeks an answer that is obvious or certain and has an expected response. An example of a leading question is "Who has control here?" There's an implied "right" answer since only the client has control instead of asking a truly open question such as "What do you want to do about the situation?"

Without sufficient context, a request can also become the coach's agenda. "Would you be willing to try this exercise?" is a leading question because the chances of your client saying no are slim to none. Clients want to comply, and in this case your client very likely surrenders to your request versus genuinely agreeing. They may feel uncomfortable, resentful, or manipulated.

If you believe an exercise might be helpful, it's important to provide context. Give an explanation as to the purpose of the exercise and why it's useful so your client has this information before making a commitment. As helpful as exercises might be, there's a price to pay if it's not fully endorsed by your client.

There are some requests that could go against the grain. "Close your eyes" isn't okay for many people. However, when you say, "There's an exercise that could help you view your situation differently. It involves closing your eyes. Are you comfortable with that?" Framing the request this way prepares your client to answer honestly.

It's important to allow the client to set the agenda but it's also your role to keep the conversation focused and moving forward. Therefore, if you *lead by following* (use what the client has offered as the basis for your question), you aren't hijacking the agenda. If it becomes your agenda for the client, the client will feel a disconnect.

THE AGREEMENT

The agreement is the point in the conversation where you and the client agree on what the focus will be and what outcome makes sense.

I firmly believe that the question, "What do you want to focus on?" during the conversation is one of *timing*. When looking at the specific situation, and the client's long-term plan, this is a tricky and oftentimes contentious point.

Sometimes that question needs to come well into the conversation, allowing time for a specific and appropriate direction for the coaching to become apparent. Pushing for a response early on only causes frustration. Within the first ten minutes or so of a conversation there is *usually* a natural place to say, "Based on where we are, what would be helpful for the rest of this conversation?" or "What will be most helpful at this point?" That said, there is no set timeframe for establishing and deepening the agreement. In some sessions it won't become really clear what your client desires until far into the conversation.

The agreement needs to go deeper than the answer to one simple question. Because the agreement is so vital to the conversation, it requires further exploration. There are several questions that can help to solidify the agreement, such as:

- What is important about accomplishing X?
- What is significant about X?
- What do you think would be helpful to achieve X?
- What will help you know that you have achieved X?
- What will X look like once you achieve it?

It's important to remember that both you and your client must be clear about the purpose of the coaching. If at any time it seems as though the conversation is veering in a different direction, it's imperative to start the agreement process again.

Let's look at the conventional approach and then how the Laser-Focused approach might deal with establishing the agreement as demonstrated on a group mentor call.

* * *

Jean: I have this situation — as you already know, I broke up with my boyfriend about six months ago and it completely caught me off guard. He sent me an email about three weeks ago saying he's coming back to town and wants to get together for coffee. It took me a while to figure out — do I want to go or not? — but I let him know that it would be fine. And then he never emailed me again, and I'm sitting here, I have all of his stuff still in my house, and I don't know what to do with it.

Here's the conventional approach with Jean:

Coach: Hi, how're you doing?

Jean: I'm doing pretty okay.

Coach: Jean, what can we talk about today?

Jean: (above story)

Coach: So you want to figure out what to do with all his stuff. What kind of outcome do you want from this conversation?

Jean: I want clarity to know what the right thing to do is after six months.

Coach: Why do you think you want to know about the right thing?

Jean: Well, because I sort of feel responsible for giving it back. On the other hand, he's kind of a jerk and I still have a lot of resentment.

Coach: How will you know that we figured out what you need in this conversation?

Jean: I guess by having clarity at the end, a plan of action of what to do with his stuff.

Coach: Great, let's definitely work toward a plan. You're not very happy with this guy, and he's in your life again. So how does that feel?

Jean: I'm a little bit confused. I thought I had resolved everything. But then when the email came for coffee, I started realizing I still feel pretty pissed about what happened.

Coach: What do you think is making you so angry about it?

Jean: I just didn't feel that he ended it right. I feel like he could have been more respectful of our relationship, and I feel like I never got to say what I wanted to say about it.

Coach: Why don't you think about calling him, or maybe when you get together you can have that opportunity? What do you think?

Jean: Oh, yeah. I actually started thinking I should go so I can really tell him what I think. That's a great idea.

Coach: That sounds great.

Here's the Laser-Focused approach with Jean:

Coach: Hi, how're you doing?

Jean: I'm doing pretty okay.

Coach: Oh, so only "pretty okay." So that has me curious. In our time together, what is it that we can focus on that will be helpful for you?

Jean: (above story)

Coach: What I'm getting from this, Jean, is that even though this relationship ended quite some time back, it sounds like there's still something going on between you because there's going to be a meeting. So, I wonder, what are you hoping to accomplish in getting together again?

Jean: I've gone through everything from "Well, maybe it will just bring me closure" to "Maybe I really need to tell him exactly how I feel" to "Maybe there's still a spark there." I have to be honest; I've thought all different kinds of things. I don't know if it's a smart thing to do, or not a smart thing to do. It could go so many possible ways.

Coach: What has you in this questioning mode?

Jean: Well, I feel like I've done a lot of growing and healing over these last few months, and I really felt that I was getting to a place of closure, and I don't want to get sucked back in and do the wrong thing that could bring up all the sadness and regret that I've been experiencing.

Coach: It sounds like the fear underneath is that if you do get together again, it may disturb some of the healing process that's already taken place. **What, then, would be really helpful for us to look at now in this conversation?**

Jean: Well, I thought it was about the stuff, but the reality is I want to feel as if I'm making the right decisions for the right reasons. I want to know what the best thing for me is versus worrying about what he is thinking or trying to prove or show. So what's the right thing for me?

Coach: What is coming up for you even as you ask, "What's the right thing for me?"

Jean: I realize that a lot of times I do things for other people. And that's one thing that just sort of clicked for me: how often I will do things to not have people upset with me or to show that I'm really strong. Part of what's coming up for me is that the past is the past, and I know it's not the right relationship even though I was very hurt by it.

Coach: What does that mean, then, in terms of what you want from this conversation?

Jean: I think it could go a couple of different ways. But I really want to explore what it is that I want, how to handle interacting with him, and what I want to say. And some kind of boundaries or something, having to do with him. I guess a side note is to figure out what to do with his stuff so I can feel separate and independent because we're not in a relationship anymore.

Coach: Something I did hear was this tendency to want to look out for the other person instead of just yourself. In this particular scenario, where you've got this ended relationship and now the possibility of seeing this person again, if there were no consequences and there were no feelings involved, what exactly would you really want in this situation?

Jean: I think what I want is a strong need to be heard about how blindsided I was. I'd like to be able to communicate that, and to ask a few questions about it. And I'd like to be able to move on with my life.

Coach: One thing, Jean, that I've seen in my experience is that you can ask all the questions you want, but you may not get honest answers. While it may feel as though you're getting what you need, there has to be a bigger reason for even wanting this conversation, because it may or may not happen the way you want. What do you think that might be?

Jean: Yeah, and I guess if I felt heard and felt like I could communicate what I really wanted to, or get answers, it would feel like closure. And closure meaning not that wondering of "Why?" and "How come?" But you're right; the answer may never be the right answer. That's true.

Coach: If that's in fact the case, it sounds like you have it in your mind that this might be the only way to get the closure that you feel you need. What might be some other options?

After listening, here are some comments from the other coaches on the group mentor call:

Conventional approach: It sounded like a prescribed formula and stayed within the story. The coach accepted what Jean said and stayed on the track without exploration. The questions stayed at the surface and went to problem-solving. There was a "why" question asking for justification.

Laser-Focused approach: Right away the coach picked up on Jean's tone and description ("pretty okay"). Notice how much exploration took place before approaching the agreement. And when Jean's response didn't answer the question, the question had to be repeated. Note how everything the coach asked was in response to what Jean said and nothing was glossed over. Every question was about Jean, not the situation.

As you may surmise from this chapter, the beginning of a conversation often determines the depth of the coaching and promotes efficiency and effectiveness right from the start. Having looked at making the beginning questions meaningful, let's look at making all of the questions impactful throughout the conversation.

QUESTIONS FOR REFLECTION

- What do you think about this anatomy of a conversation compared to your current approach?
- What might change in your approach based on the information that the first question after your client's story determines the depth of the conversation?
- What comes to mind when you think about postponing the agreement?

CHAPTER 5

THE ART OF THE QUESTION

Being heard is so close to being loved that for the average person they are almost indistinguishable.
— David Augsburger

Masterful coaches ask open, thought-provoking questions to understand the person. The questions force the client to think rather than provide information they already know. There are certain types of questions that help to get right to the heart of a client's situation, and others that lead to dead ends or irrelevant information. In this chapter, you'll discover how to consistently frame powerful questions so that the client has to do all of the thinking instead of you. Questioning this way diminishes the client's storytelling and gets deeper information by going right to the heart.

Building trust is crucial and one of the easiest ways to do that is to let the client feel heard. To do this, start with reflection, followed by a short question.

BE A REFLECTOR, NOT A PARROT

There are several instances during a conversation and especially after the opening story, when it helps to let the client know you understand what they are saying. This is referred to as reflection. Newer coaches tend to parrot or mirror information back to clients in an attempt to demonstrate that they're listening. The conversation might sound like this:

Client: When my boss criticized me in front of the CEO, I was devastated. How could she do that to me after all I've done for her?

Coach: When your boss criticized you in front of the CEO, you were devastated and wondered how she could do that after all you've done for her. How did you handle it?

A seasoned coach reflects with less precision and includes empathy. Consider this response: "It makes sense that you were deeply upset when your boss threw you under the bus, especially since you go out of your way to help her. What might be helpful based on this?"

Your client doesn't need to go into detail or to hear their exact words spat back at them. There are exceptions when they use unique words or expressions, but overall your role is to reflect, not repeat.

> *Reflection can be thought of as **encapsulating the essence**, and if possible, the emotion of what your client shared.*

Here are some basic benefits of reflection:

- It's important to establish rapport and trust. Reflection helps your client feel heard and understood.
- Sometimes the client is surprised that what they said came across the way you reflected it back to them thus opening up discussion opportunities.
- It lets you and your client know you're on the same page.

When you hear data from your client and reflect it back, you're sharing your interpretation of the data, which can be very helpful. Since your objective is to get the best understanding possible, any data is welcome. Your reflection is the meaning that you, as the coach, ascribe to your client's words. It's the overall observation, gist, idea, or theme of what you, as the outside, objective listener gets

68

from their words. If your interpretation isn't accurate, your client will gladly supply the correct data. It's critical that you, as the coach, own your observation rather than declare it as truth for your client.

Instead of saying, "You sound betrayed by your boss, right?" own the observation as your interpretation and then check for agreement: "It seems there's a feeling of being betrayed by your boss. What's true about that?" Keep in mind that it's your interpretation and not necessarily what is actually going on with your client. After an observation, it is imperative to include a brief question to allow them to respond to your interpretation.

Reflection creates clarity about what's going on with your client, which is important because you don't want to:

- Take the wrong coaching path
- Make assumptions or guesses about what's going on with your client
- Inadvertently create your own agenda
- Create a disconnect because your client doesn't feel heard and understood

When reflecting back to your client, what is most important is that they feel as though you understand who they are and have learned something about them. It can be helpful to include something about their values, characteristics, or emotions. Aim to find a balance between your client feeling heard and your interpretation without getting into their story.

* * *

Tessa shared that she went to her favorite art supply store to order new brushes. The clerk ignored her and continued looking at her phone. Tessa cleared her throat and the clerk snapped, "I can't help you now," and left the register to speak to another customer at the back of the store. Tessa moved to the brush display and started looking for what she needed even though she was certain the store did not carry that specific brush. When another clerk came to the register, Tessa asked for help and the second clerk put in an order for the brush she required.

A new coach might reflect:

"It sounds like the first clerk didn't value you."
(This reflection is not focused on Tessa but on the clerk.)

Or,

"I'm surprised you didn't give up and move on."
(This reflection comes across as very judgmental, as if persevering was a bad thing.)

Or,

"You sounded relieved at the end."
(This reflection accuses Tessa of what she was feeling rather than holding it as the coach's opinion.)

A seasoned coach might reflect:

"It seems as though your value as a customer was disregarded, and yet your patience and tenacity paid off in the end. What comes to mind hearing this?"
(This reflection focuses on Tessa and her character and allows her to feel heard and understood.)

Client-centered, empathetic reflection is powerful and is always followed by an open question to allow the client an opportunity to share their thoughts.

"NOSEY" CURIOSITY VERSUS COACHING CURIOSITY

Before going into the specifics around framing powerful questions, it's important to distinguish "nosey" curiosity versus coaching curiosity.

"Nosey" curiosity is when you're asking a question for *your* benefit, not the client's. It is when you're curious about something the client already knows, so their answer is only for you and doesn't move the conversation forward. "What did you say when you heard that?" — the client already knows what they said! An example of coaching curiosity: "What was it like for you when you heard that?" The answer is something your client hasn't already thought about or expressed and will elicit relevant data. True coaching curiosity addresses the client's thoughts and feelings that provide relevant data that distinctly move the conversation forward.

It can often seem like you need more data, more details to better understand what's going on.

> *You never need the "back story" —
> the history or background.*

Your client will nearly always provide all the detail you need at the start of the conversation even if it doesn't seem so.

An exception might be when your client provides insufficient data such as "I'm thinking about leaving my job." You have no clue where this thought is coming from and might ask, "What's prompting this thought at this point in time?" (Avoid: Tell me more...) The client may or may not be clear on what's prompting the statement but hasn't provided sufficient data for clear understanding.

Now that we've established what it means to approach questions with coaching curiosity, let's look at some key principles for framing powerful questions.

ASK "WHAT" QUESTIONS

Asking "What" questions as opposed to "How" and "Why" questions almost always yields more pertinent data and prevents clients from going deeper into their story. You might think that's crazy, but I'm inviting you to give it a try before dismissing the idea.

71

A "What" question becomes incredibly powerful when it forces the client to think about something in a new way, rather than tell you something they already know.

"What" questions are open and look toward the future (What do you...? What does that mean? What makes this important?), whereas "How" questions usually ask for a description or method (How would you...? How is this important?) while "Why" questions typically ask for justification (Why did you...? Why would you...?). Because the typical response to a "Why" question starts with "Because" and goes into the past, it can easily make your client feel defensive.

I learned this concept from Laura Berman Fortgang in the mid-1990s. Her term is "Wisdom Access Questions," because wisdom is exactly what "What" questions elicit.

It can seem awkward at first to reword your questions starting with "What," but with practice and perseverance you will notice a *significant and relevant difference* in your clients' responses. This is true in both your personal and professional life. You probably won't use "What" questions 100 percent of the time, but if you can get into the habit, you will observe that your coaching is elevated almost instantly based on the responses.

Every question should force your client to think.

Note the distinctions:

- "*Why* did you choose this conference?"
  The response will likely begin with "Because" and will likely sound defensive. The question looks to the past and can sound judgmental. The response might be something like, "Because it seemed important for my career," which you both already know; it doesn't elicit any new data.

- "*How* did you choose this conference?"

  The response will likely involve methodology: "I looked at the options and decided it was the only time I could leave my family," or "I checked out the speakers and decided it would bring a lot of value." Again, it doesn't yield new data or move the conversation forward. "How" is better used near the end of a coaching conversation when you want to ascertain the method of how something will be accomplished or executed.

- "*What* do you expect to gain from this conference?"

  The response will yield relevant data, go into more depth, and generate forward thinking: "I'm hoping to meet people to do my joint venture project, to network and get new clients, and to get new information that will help me become more efficient at work."

> *When you question the situation, your*
> *client will go deeper into the story.*
> *When you question the person,*
> *you invite thinking.*

ASK OPEN-ENDED QUESTIONS

One of the most valuable things a coach does is to ask powerful questions that move the conversation forward. "What do you mean by that?" might be the most impactful question of the entire conversation. The simplest question can be the most powerful because of its timing. In addition to starting with "What," each question should be open-ended. A closed question could yield a simple yes or no, and then you have to think of the next question.

> *The coach should never have to think.*
> *Rather ask open questions that force the*
> *client to do the thinking.*

Note the difference in the following responses:

Question: Did you think it was important?

Answer: Yes, somewhat. (or No, not really.)

Question: What was important to you about that?

Answer: It reminded me of something that happened a while ago that impacted my life. When I thought about it, I realized exactly what I need to do now with this situation.

Notice how the open question is likely to give you new data. The closed question rarely gives you any significant data, forcing you to think instead of the client.

Coaches frequently say, "Say more about that," or "Tell me more." Both these expressions sound a bit like a command, and more often than not invite irrelevant details that don't move the conversation forward. If you feel compelled to ask for more, it's far more invitational to ask, "What else can you say about that?"

How do you automatically make your questions open and elicit meaningful data?

ADD CONTEXT TO QUESTIONS

When you ask questions during coaching conversations, it's often important to provide context, otherwise the question can sound like it's coming from left field, can be perceived as judgmental, or just doesn't make sense.

Consider this personal experience from many years ago:

* * *

While on vacation with a friend, I noticed he was folding a blanket in a strange way. I asked him, "Why are you folding the blanket that way?" His reply: "I hate when you ask those kinds of questions!" After attempting to understand what that meant, and not getting a response, I had to let it go.

Later that evening, while in the midst of a meaningful conversation, he asked, "Marion, what's your bra size?" Totally taken aback, I asked why he would ask me that kind of question at that point in time. He replied, "So that you know what it feels like to get a question with no context."

While coaching, it's important to share where a question comes from. Apparently, my question came across as judgmental because there was no context. If I had said, "I'm intrigued by the way you're folding that blanket. I've never seen anyone do it that way. Where did you learn that?" I likely would have gotten a response.

This experience helped me realize that we have so much going on in our minds that we often don't provide enough context, we just ask the question. There's no reflection, no thread, no connection to what's been said.

I refer to this as a "naked" question. There are times when it's okay to just ask a question, but more often than not, there should be a thread that weaves your client's response with your question.

Lead by following. In other words, use what the client just said as the lead into your question. Too often, a client shares a few sentences or tells a long story and the coach asks a simplistic question that implies that they weren't really listening, or it doesn't provide context for answering. This doesn't necessarily mean ask about the last thing said but rather encapsulate the entire gist.

For instance, a client might say, "I had such a hard time with my co-worker. She seemed irritated with me because I wouldn't help her finish her project when I was just trying to get through my own work. Now I worry about having created problems in our relationship," and the coach asks, "What do you want to do about it?" as opposed to "Working together every day makes the relationship important. What would you like to do about it?"

Then there's the "it" problem. A client might say, "The report was so challenging, and I couldn't figure out how to do it. It was too difficult for me," and the coach asks, "What made it difficult?" Now the client thinks, "What was too difficult?" Clients rarely remember what they just said.

Instead of asking what made *it* difficult, "What made the report so difficult for you?" provides not only context (the report), but also will likely yield a much better response to add to your databank.

ASK SHORT AND BROAD QUESTIONS

While listening, thoughts may come up in your mind and you will want to cram all of those thoughts into your next question. However, this is different from providing context that precedes the question. In particular, I am talking about what is included in the question.

If a client is concerned about the length of a presentation and the coach asks, "Would you like it more if it was shorter or longer?" the client is now compelled to make a choice. We don't want to tie clients into choosing. Instead, if the question is totally open and thought-provoking, it might sound like, "What impact does the length have to do with it?"

Questions can also get too wordy and become diluted. Compare a question such as "What impact would you like to have on your boss when you hand in your project and show him how much you have accomplished?" to "When handing in your project to your boss, what impact are you hoping to have?" Which do you think is more likely to provide you with good data? If we get too wordy, the client has a hard time remembering all our points, making it hard for them to respond.

The less specific the question, the better. This allows the client to answer in whatever way comes to mind. Note this comparison: "What is better for you, to drop the art class or muddle through it?" Or "What would be the best thing to do right now?" The second question is broad, simple, and open. It doesn't present narrow choices or direction.

* * *

Anne returned for coaching when she retired from her twenty-five years as a math teacher. She is pursuing her next career as a financial planner. She reports: "Despite my great qualifications, no one is responding to my resume, and I think it's because they tend toward hiring men. I've read that being a woman in this field is a problem, but I'm not really sure if my gender is what is holding me back."

The types of questions that I hear after this type of scenario are things like:

- "What has you choosing financial planning?"
- "How do you know that being a woman in this field is a problem?"

Instead, a simple question such as "What do you think?" is short and broad and doesn't require any thinking. The question puts her doubts back on her because she's isn't sure that gender is the problem. When she responds to "What do you think?" she says things like "Maybe I'm not as qualified as I think" or "Perhaps being a teacher doesn't really translate to becoming a financial planner," etc. The question is so simple, but it has her thinking that there may be reasons besides gender rather than asking her to justify her choice or provide evidence of her hunch.

Without realizing it, questions can come across as judgmental or contain an assumption. For example, "What bothers you most about that?" *assumes* the client is bothered. Instead consider, "What, if anything, bothers you the most?" Just adding "if anything" takes out any assumption of how the client is feeling.

There is no need for a list of questions. The simplest question at the right time may be the most powerful of all.

AVOID STACKED QUESTIONS

Frequently we ask a question and then think of a better one or a better way to say it, so we ask it in another way: "What does that mean? What will you do? What comes up for you?" This is called stacking questions and unfortunately, the client hears only the last one.

Ironically, most often the first question was the best one. Even if you don't like your question, rather than stacking another one right after it, let it stick and allow the client to answer. In this way, it will be easier for the client to stay in partnership with you. Hold in mind that the client doesn't distinguish between "great" and "mediocre" questions.

QUESTIONS FOR REFLECTION

- What will be different as you learn to reflect when appropriate before a question?
- What comes to mind when you think about providing/ not providing context for your questions?
- What might be tricky or uncomfortable about mainly using "What" questions?

PART III:
THE MIDDLE

CHAPTER 6

DON'T BELIEVE THE CLIENT

There were many terrible things in my life and
most of them never happened.
— Michel de Montaigne

It's helpful to understand human behavior, recognize underlying themes, and laser in on what matters most. The middle portion of the coaching conversation consists of getting closer to the client's truth and listening for discrepancies and underlying beliefs. This leads to creating shifts in thinking followed by "looping." Let's look at the middle section in more detail in the next few chapters.

Having gone into depth about questioning, now we will go deeper and learn new ways to hone listening skills. The first step begins with a simple, inconceivable concept: Don't believe the client.

THE ANATOMY OF A COACHING CONVERSATION			
	THE BEGINNING	THE MIDDLE	THE END
Laser-Focused Mindset	1) Opening question 2) Client story 3) First question *after story* 4) Agreement	5) Discerning truth from perception 6) The shift / change in perspective 7) Looping	8) Optional bonus question 9) Support (resources) 10) Closing and championing

DISCERN TRUTH FROM PERCEPTION

It often startles coaches to hear, "Don't believe the client." And it should.

Our clients don't lie. Everything they tell us, as far as they're concerned, is the truth. And yet often coaches find discrepancies

81

and something underneath the words as the conversation develops and discover that the client's initial story is just the tip of the iceberg. If you think about where conversations begin and where they wind up, you realize that much of the initial portion was filled with perception.

When a client complains bitterly about their job, it can turn out that their marriage, or something else, isn't working; their job is simply a by-product of a deeper frustration. Focusing on finding the truth is the basis for all that follows.

> *Until, and unless, you get to the bottom-line truth for your client, you are merely providing a band-aid.*

A masterful coach knows that life is complex and knowing precisely what a client wants and needs at any moment is challenging. Masterful coaching goes beyond the temporary strategies to focus on deeper, permanent, long-term shifts in perspective. Being able to differentiate between truth and perception allows that focus to happen.

Most of what a client tells us is based on their perceptions; they think the perceptions are true, but as outside, objective observers we realize they are not necessarily *the* truth, or the only truth for that person. However, if a client talks about having been abused by their parents every day, we don't need to question it as the literal truth but can surmise that they had a bad childhood.

Based on the following example, let's look at how to separate the truth from perception. I invite you to read the story twice and write down or note only the facts. Then continue to find out how few facts the story contains.

* * *

Will, twenty-five, tells his coach that he has tried out for the Dolphins football team for the last three years. He says that all of his life he wanted to be a football player and

82

no matter how close he gets he is continually rejected. He goes on to say that, although he is in the best shape and can run faster than most of the other players, most of the coaches just don't like him. He says that they feel a little threatened by him.

What are the *only* facts in the story?

- Will is twenty-five years old.
- He has tried out for the Dolphins football team for the last three years.
- He hasn't made the team.

Everything else is Will's perception. We have no idea how long he has wanted to play, how he compares to the other players, or how the coaches view him.

In every situation there are potentially a great deal of assumptions, and as a coach, you can become quite invested and believe them. To reframe the client's perceptions properly, you can use only the existing facts (without distortion). In this case, some possible questions that don't make Will wrong are:

- What if the Dolphins aren't the right team for you?
- What if you're trying out for the wrong position for your strengths?
- What if the coach is looking for a certain personality type to fit in with the team and is not as interested in the skills of the player?

You have to use caution to not make Will wrong or try to convince him of something. A question that would make Will wrong is, "What if you aren't as good as you think you are?" A question that tries to convince him of something is, "Is it possible that you have the wrong idea about the coaches not liking you?"

Your role is to not believe your client's interpretation as the *only* truth. Avoid getting trapped by making assumptions or drawing conclusions early on and then getting stuck in the story because you believe it to be true. As long as you're skeptical and question thoughts and ideas, you are more likely to get to the truth of what's really going on rather than your client's interpretation of the truth. Even if what your client shares seems true to you, it's only what they're *choosing* to tell.

It's important to distinguish facts from perceptions. However, you must honor your client's statements as true to them, never expressing that you don't believe them. Instead, use questions to figure out what is real, where their perceptions are coming into play, and what else might be possible.

* * *

Stan had been discussing his job frustrations for quite some time. He began one conversation by saying, "Unless I deal with my work life, I don't think it makes sense to discuss my personal challenges."

If you immediately accept his assessment, you could be missing important data such as the overlap or correlation between his work life and his personal challenges.

The more skeptical you can be and the more you can resist accepting everything stated at face value, the more masterful your coaching will be. This is contrary to what many of you learned in training. Yet if you really examine what your client is saying, it's often (though of course not always) more perception than fact.

Unconscious bias could be another factor in their difference in perception. In almost every story you'll find some element of unconscious bias coming into play. These biases lead to forming beliefs, and when we identify the beliefs behind the bias, we can help clients recognize and change those beliefs.

Think of people who've complained to you about a particular person when your experience of that person is completely different. Their complaints could be pointing to their biases. For example, if they complain that their employee is lazy, it could tell you they have strongly held beliefs around what it means to be lazy. Instead of taking their complaint at face value, we can ask questions to bring awareness such as, "What does lazy mean to you?" This opens the door to examine their beliefs instead of assuming they're right or staying stuck in their unconscious biases.

Another instance when "Don't believe the client" works well is near the end of a conversation. You might assume a conversation is complete or ask your client, "Is this a good place to stop?" When they answer "Yes," they might pause or hesitate slightly, or there might be uncertainty in their voice that needs to be addressed.

This is a good time to be skeptical and question if, in fact, the conversation *really* is complete. Every conversation should end collaboratively, with you checking in with your client and making sure they're ready to end.

As human beings, most of us tend to stick to one interpretation of the facts. As a coach, that can be detrimental. Combining the "don't believe your client" approach with simple, open questions helps to open up your client's thinking and have them see other possibilities and interpretations. It's amazing how people can be catapulted forward because they're no longer hanging on so tightly to a certain interpretation that doesn't serve them.

THE TRAFFIC HELICOPTER APPROACH

As a coach listening to your client's words, one of the most difficult things is to discern what is *really* going on. The details are seductive, and both coach and client can become sidetracked and go off on irrelevant tangents away from the heart of the matter. After all, what is the main point or reason for the story in the first place?

People want to be heard and understood. In conversation, we do this by drawing a picture for the listener and providing examples of how we came to our observations, perspectives, and conclusions, even though all the details don't necessarily enhance or clarify the information. Because we are invested in our own reasoning behind the "story," it's challenging to make a point concisely because we believe that each thing we say is necessary and relevant.

Coaching becomes meaningful when we focus on what is important about the person, their behaviors and feelings, not the myriad details about the situation that keep the client stuck. Once we shift and refine our focus, the details and tangents become inconsequential because we know how to listen beyond the words for the big picture.

One simple way to remember to stay focused on your client instead of the story is to use the "Traffic Helicopter Approach."

- How would you describe the way it hovers while inspecting the scene below?
- How does a traffic helicopter reporter share information from their vantage point?

"Being in the helicopter" means staying "above" your client's story to get the biggest picture possible. Using this vantage point, you can observe the landscape and see the patterns or themes presented in the conversation. You can choose when to hover in for a closer look to discover where your client is stuck, what thinking is creating the turmoil or conflict, and/or what thoughts are limiting their progress. Then you can go back to a high-level view and avoid being distracted or drawn in by the details. This makes it easier to ascertain what is really going on and what aspects of the story are truly pertinent and meaningful.

A traffic reporter observes the big picture so they can briefly describe the situation in a way that people immediately know where there is a problem. If there's an accident on Highway 101, it's reported as a crash in the right lane causing cars to shift to the center and far left. Or we might hear about a crash in the center lane causing a backup for miles, therefore avoid highway X and use alternate route Z. You never hear a traffic reporter describe a scene like this:

"A red SUV in the right lane with four passengers on Highway 101 was involved in a crash with a blue pick-up truck with furniture in the back and Kansas license plates and has a flat tire and is badly dented. It looks as though the truck will have to be towed, and it seems like one of the passengers from the SUV may be injured."

The traffic helicopter view allows the coach to:

- Stay focused on the person, not their situation or anyone else in the story.
- Not get sucked into details that are distracting and irrelevant.

Suppose your client shares that his wife isn't feeling well and will have to go the hospital, and he will be absent from work. The typical response might be, "Sorry to hear that, Jim. I hope she's okay. Do they have an idea of what's wrong with her?" However, holding in mind "Why is he telling me this?" he might really be saying that he is worried about his wife's health, the implications for his children, and how he would care for them on his own. Or he could be fearful about having to take time off from work and losing pay. There may be concerns underneath that simple statement that could be easily dismissed or misunderstood if the coach doesn't get the big picture of Jim's anxiety and how he will handle his responsibilities.

In this situation, a masterful coach avoids asking about the details of the wife's illness. Asking him if he would like to talk about it is an invitation. By staying in the helicopter, you can help Jim explore the underlying feelings and thoughts behind his statement, keeping the focus squarely on him.

* * *

Judy begins the conversation saying, "I'm so frustrated. No matter how many times I explain to my boss that his way of handling new projects and not discussing what he expects is driving me crazy, he doesn't change. Just the other day, he gave me this huge, complex project and rather than explaining it and making sure I understood what is expected, he puts a short note saying, "I need this by Tuesday. I'm busy and don't have time, so do the best you can."

It's the type of situation where you want to "fix" the problem and help Judy get a satisfying solution. Your initial inclination might be to ask something like, "What do you want him to do instead?" The problem with this question is it's focused on "the other" person, not Judy. Another typical question might be, "Is this project similar to anything else you've done before so you could draw on past experience?" This question asks for more detail and story and neither question addresses the problem. No matter what her boss does or what she's done before, she needs help finding a way she can either stay in her position with less frustration or choose to leave. Although her boss could use some management skills, he is irrelevant in the conversation.

In this case, the helicopter view: Judy is unhappy, her boss isn't changing, and Judy has to decide what she wants to do. We don't need any information about the projects or what she has told her boss. It's all about Judy and what she wants to do going forward — not the boss and not the projects.

GETTING BACK INTO THE HELICOPTER

Getting sucked into the story is very common. The Traffic Helicopter Approach takes practice to master. When you notice that you're bogged down in the details or your focus is off your client, you can refocus. Here are some helpful ways to get back in the helicopter:

- Reflect on something you heard and ask a question about your client (not their situation).
- Look for the emotion — while you never want to *dwell* in feelings or emotions, it's extremely helpful to *identify* your client's emotion because, in the end, that's what changes. The types of emotions that are helpful to identify are frustration, annoyance, confusion, disappointment, overwhelm, etc.

- Hold in mind the two critical questions discussed in Chapter 3: "Why are they telling me this?" and "What's making this a problem for them?"

At times you may encounter your own distracting thoughts, doubts, and confusion. Just notice them and return your attention to focusing on your client. As you gain more experience using transformational techniques, those distractions and doubts become less frequent.

By staying "above the fray" and out of the details, we can more easily get to the bottom-line truth and help a client gain a new perspective.

Now that we've looked at some foundational components of discerning truth from perception, in the next chapter we'll go deeper by exploring how we can further discern and leverage truth.

QUESTIONS FOR REFLECTION

- What will be different going forward if you don't take your client's initial perspective at face value?
- What can you do to remind yourself to stay in the helicopter and avoid getting lost in the details of a story?
- What might change when you're able to distinguish a truth from a perception?

CHAPTER 7

UNDERSTANDING HUMAN BEHAVIOR

*If you carry the bricks from your past relationships
to the new one, you will build the same house.*
— lifelifehappy.com

As clients go deeper into their stories, it's helpful for us to keep a broad perspective and look beyond the immediate story they share. To do this, we need to understand human behavior. This enables us to recognize patterns and get to the heart of their story more quickly.

In this chapter, you'll discover a powerful methodology that uses basic principles of human behavior called Structural Alignment™. This information (shared with permission) was created and developed by Tony A. Kirkland, MS, in the early 1990s to understand human behavior more deeply. It has been extremely powerful and significant as background information for my coaching and that of my students.

Laser-Focused Coaching is about getting to the client's truth. For clients to create their lives the way they want, it is helpful to understand what it takes to make that happen as well as the reasons why clients may not be progressing. Structural Alignment helps you and your client align intention with action, resulting in powerful progress.

91

Structural Alignment is based on the alignment of truth, vision, purpose, and spirituality so that there is no room for conflict, and everything flows in a forward-moving direction. Conflict or struggle occurs when any one of these elements is misaligned.

It helps clients transform their view of the world and themselves, while uncovering patterns in their thinking and behavior. When you understand Structural Alignment, you can avoid getting trapped in your client's story, which typically results in a temporary solution. Rather, you'll be able to focus solely on your client as a whole person, and thereby create a long-lasting or permanent shift in perspective and allow them to live authentically.

Structural Alignment isn't about a process of "ask this question; then ask that question," but rather provides a framework for helping your client learn about themselves, receive clarity that is aligned with their truth, and change their habitual patterns of thought and behavior. It's much more powerful and sustainable than just asking your client what they want to accomplish and moving right to goals and action steps.

It is a profound way to understand human behavior and coach masterfully because it leads to a long-term shift in perspective. Once that shift occurs, the client is empowered and able to devise their own next steps.

HOW STRUCTURAL ALIGNMENT WORKS

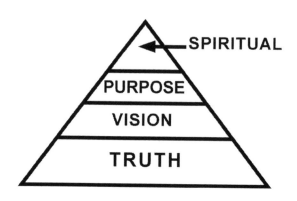

There are four levels and each one has to align in order for someone to create and live a fulfilling and authentic life. When clients present a challenge, one or more of these levels is misaligned. The levels are defined as:

Truth: The foundation necessary for a vision to be possible — reality.

Vision: A concept or view in broad strokes, or an aim or desire in designing a plan or intention; a future orientation that serves as the basis for making a decision or taking action.

Purpose: A reason for doing something; a vision that is driven by a compelling reason to exist.

Spiritual: The human spirit or soul as opposed to material or physical things. A place of true inner peace where there is harmony between body and spirit. It's sometimes referred to as the "true Self." Thus, this must align with our purpose, vision, and truth.

When you understand each level and see how they need to align, this framework will help you to understand what is keeping the client from getting exactly what they want. Each element is discussed in more depth.

Truth

> *It's not what we don't know that hurts us, people say.*
> *It's what we believe is true that isn't that does the damage.*
> — Melody Beattie

Great coaching doesn't require a specific prompt or a preconceived powerful question. Rather, figuring out what is really true for the client is masterful coaching.

Truth is the foundation of Structural Alignment and it is usually the most difficult to pin down. Therefore, the majority of time in coaching sessions should be spent ascertaining what is really true for your client.

93

The client's stated goal may not be the "'truth" for the client. It can be fraught with fear, misconceptions, and underlying beliefs that are keeping the client from achieving it. I liken this to someone saying they want the CEO position at their firm, but they're constantly overlooked. What we discover is that they have an underlying belief that CEOs are lonely, have no time for family, and have a lot of responsibilities. Until those underlying beliefs are addressed, the goal is meaningless, because for every few steps forward, the client is likely to take self-sabotaging steps backward. They might be more comfortable sitting in their current pain than they are willing to move toward their goal. The goal is often filled with fear and/or negative underlying beliefs.

If you ask the average person "What would make you happy?" you can imagine what most people would answer: "I want a million dollars. Then I could do whatever I want and not have to worry about anything." Without exploring the truth, the coach who hears this believes that their client wants a lot of money and then begins to strategize how to make that happen.

In Structural Alignment coaching, we examine the truth of that statement until it becomes apparent that money may only be one means of manifesting our client's desire. Deep down what they really want is the feeling of freedom and the ability to make better choices. Until we figure out what *experience* people want to have, versus how it might manifest, coaching simply meets goals but never truly addresses the root of their desires, and true satisfaction is not attained. Once we know the truth, we can look at various ways our client might find happiness and fulfillment, and it's not necessarily the one way they imagined.

* * *

My client, Melanie, who also happened to be a professional coach, was talking about her grown daughter and her boyfriend. She initially claimed that she wanted to tell her daughter that the boyfriend was not a good person and cited several examples of this. She claimed that she needed an opportunity to have a conversation with her daughter and share her viewpoint. In actuality, when we examined what the real truth was, it turned out it was all about Melanie's fears, hopes, and dreams for her daughter. It was about her fear that her daughter wouldn't be happy. It really wasn't about the boyfriend's traits and character, but everything to do with her relationship with her daughter and what she wanted for her. The conversation took less than thirty minutes, and Melanie totally shifted her thinking when she realized that the boyfriend aspect distracted from what was really going on.

In the above example, the question that changed everything was, "When you are in conversation with your daughter, who is the client?" In other words, Melanie had the problem, not her daughter.

Helping clients discover their deep truth provides clarity that can lead to potent change. To combat the struggle and challenge that comes from misalignment, the emphasis should be on *what's really true*, and coaches are well-positioned to help clients explore this misalignment.

The desired experience — a component of truth

We can never determine what's possible for another person. We tend to think that anything is possible, but our client's goal could be illogical or unrealistic. Coaches want to believe their clients are capable of anything, so they tend to stick with "Okay, let's go for it." An important element of truth is identifying the client's desired experience. Therefore, first we should look for the *experience* the client wants, *not how they want it to manifest.*

For example, although some people say they can't sing, I literally cannot. I have no pitch, can't carry a tune, and can't distinguish high notes from low notes. As a client I might say, "I'm

95

really not good at singing," but likely wouldn't tell you the straight-up truth — that I really, really can't sing. Let's say despite this, I hire a coach to help me fulfill my dream of becoming an opera singer. We could work on that forever, and the chances are slim to none that it will happen because it's unrealistic for me since it's not anchored in my truth. However, if a coach helped me dig deeper into that desired outcome, they could help me discover something important. What matters is finding out what experience I want to have — why an opera singer?

A question that would help the coach determine what is true might be, "What experience are you hoping to have as an opera singer?" Perhaps what I actually want to experience is the attention, the accolades, being on stage, getting applause, and feeling special. More aligned with my truth — and likely achievable — might be public speaking, teaching, or facilitating.

Vision

> *Vision without action is fantasy.*
> *Action without vision is chaos.*
> *— Michael Bernard Beckwith*

The next level in Structural Alignment is the vision. It's the broad-stroke picture of what someone wants their life to look like, such as, "I want a family, two or three children, to be happily married, to live in a house by the water, and to have part-time work that really fulfills me."

Goals have their place in coaching. However, when we're considering the whole person, goals are not necessarily the best way to get results. We cross them off our list and say, "Okay, fine, now I have to make a new goal," whereas a vision has some flexibility; it's bigger and it's broader. It encompasses everything they want, how they want it, what it looks like, what it feels like, and what it will mean for them once they have it. It might look like: "I want to work in a large corporation and have a loving family," and as time goes on, the client realizes they want to be an entrepreneur. A vision is flexible, not carved in stone.

Visions describe the overarching picture, and if they're compelling, they pull people forward. If a vision isn't compelling, the client will likely not move toward it. If it *is* compelling, the client holds their vision in front of them to remind them of *why* they are moving toward their desired outcome.

It helps you as a coach to know what your client ultimately wants, and *their vision must be anchored in their truth*. When a seventy-year-old man wants to start medical school and become a doctor, it's likely not anchored in his truth, so it's likely not going to happen. To determine the alignment of vision to truth, it's crucial to keep the whole client in mind and not their situation.

Clients often confuse the experience they want to have with how it will manifest.

* * *

Andrew said, "I want to take a year off and travel." It sounded like a goal. When I questioned him and presented it realistically, we discovered that he wanted to experience a feeling of freedom, and held the idea that travel was the only way to accomplish that.

When I discussed with Andrew that travel means a lot of moving around, unpacking and repacking and not seeing friends and family regularly, he realized that something wasn't quite right with his travel goal. He had only traveled a bit in the past, but each time he felt freedom from the pressures at work. That relief of pressure was what he really wanted, not a year living in hotels. If I had blindly accepted that the goal was to travel for a year, within a short time he would have returned feeling unsatisfied and perhaps disappointed. Clearly, there are other ways to experience the feeling of freedom.

Purpose

> *The two most important days in your*
> *life are the day you are born and*
> *the day you find out why.*
> — Mark Twain

The next level up in Structural Alignment is purpose. To discover our purpose is to discover why we're here on this planet, what our gifts are, and what we're meant to do with our lives.

Everyone wants to find meaning in their lives. Some think of it as their legacy or unique contribution to the world. While the language may differ, we all have the desire to live a meaningful life.

Without a sense of purpose, we wander aimlessly. Conversely, when we contribute to a higher purpose, we are fulfilled. When people work in jobs that feel meaningless to them, each day is a struggle because it isn't aligned with what they are truly meant to be doing. If we think about any professional who feels engaged and satisfied, it is because they are living a purposeful life.

Just as I began this book with my personal story of awareness, at the same time, I also realized that my purpose is to share my knowledge and experience with others. One way to help identify your purpose is to ask yourself what it is about you that makes you special to other people and what do they appreciate about you. In many cases, the answer is your (or your client's) purpose.

Purpose, in turn, must align with truth and vision. If it's your truth and aligns with what you want and stems from your purpose, life feels smooth and fulfilling.

If you notice that a client isn't progressing, and yet their vision is anchored in their truth, it is an opportunity to explore their purpose as that may not be aligned.

When purpose is not aligned with vision and truth:

* * *

Dwight had always planned to be a lawyer. He went to the finest law school and was highly successful. But deep in his heart he knew this was not what he wanted. His real desire was to travel the world, teach in other countries, and help the poor. However, it felt too impractical and others depended on his financial success.

Despite Dwight's successful career, it wasn't rooted in purpose. When a client's heart isn't in something, they have an unmet desire to contribute, or they feel unfulfilled, these are clues that their purpose is missing. In this case, he needed to find a way to reconcile the truth of where his life was and create a new vision that aligned with his desire to serve the poor (purpose). This led him to realigning his law practice to serving disadvantaged victims of the legal system.

Spiritual

The top level of the Structural-Alignment pyramid is our *real* self, absent of ego, where we are not influenced by experience, history, environment, or our persona. When this aligns with our purpose, vision, and truth, we are living our best life.

Spirituality means the true Self — beyond anything tangible, material, or physical. It's a way of expressing our *higher selves* and feeling a profound sense of belonging. In its purest form, the spiritual is a sense of completion and true peace that is guided and connected by something greater than oneself. Not necessarily on a conscious level, clients seek coaching because they believe there is a potentially more fulfilling reality.

A client can be aligned in the first three levels, but a lack of spiritual alignment leads to harm. Some of the greatest atrocities in history were rooted in truths that involved intolerance for certain people, visions about how to handle those people, and a deep-seated sense of purpose that they were doing the right thing.

Unfortunately, their alignment in the first three levels made them quite successful in achieving their desires. What was missing was the level of spiritual alignment that ultimately led to the downfall of these agendas and caused great damage in the process.

In the context of Structural Alignment, the spiritual means that everything the client is working towards is rooted in compassion, consideration, connection, and generosity. When it is, success is easy to sustain and benefits everyone. In the highly unlikely event that you notice a client's desires might cause harm or are rooted in ill will or anger, obviously coaching isn't appropriate.

Along with aligning truth, vison, purpose, and spirituality, another important aspect of coaching is understanding human behavior and how it shows up in our clients. As we move into the next chapter on themes, keeping Structural Alignment in mind, you will notice it gets easier to keep the big picture in mind and not get trapped by details.

QUESTIONS FOR REFLECTION

- What difference will becoming familiar with Structural Alignment have in your coaching?
- What about the distinction between goals and vision intrigues you?
- What will be the impact of knowing that the experience a client wants may supersede the way they envision how it will manifest?

CHAPTER 8

USING THEMES TO SEE THE BIG PICTURE

Growth is painful. Change is painful. But nothing is as painful as staying stuck somewhere you don't belong.
— Unknown

We are well acquainted with themes in literature and movies, such as *crime doesn't pay, coming of age, overcoming the odds, love conquers all,* etc. Just as stories have themes, so does coaching. They show up as the overarching way a client thinks about their life, challenges, and desires. Each coaching conversation has at least one theme, if not several.

When you recognize a theme, you will know exactly what is needed to help your client make a profound, permanent change in their perspective. This keeps you out of the details of their story and into Laser-Focused Coaching no matter how little or how much coaching experience you have, thus helping your client permanently transform their thinking.

What belief about life is the client actually conveying when describing their circumstances? The theme is generally expressed through the client's actions, words, and thoughts. The most powerful coaches move quickly beyond the stories and delve into the themes.

This chapter introduces the twenty-five common themes that appear in coaching conversations. It will help you to create a "theme cheat sheet" making it easy to identify them. Themes help inform the coach as to what powerful questions to ask about the person, not the situation.

When we were in grade school, we focused on a story's details and events, known as the plot. Making the distinction between the plot of the story (what) and the person (who) is crucial. Coaches often get seduced by the plot. After all, the story has lots of juicy details, so it takes skill and practice to learn how to bypass the plot and focus on the theme.

When you understand and think in terms of themes, there's no need to take a lot of notes, and the story with its many details pales in significance compared to the overriding belief that drives the client's behavior.

* * *

Alex came to a coaching session with three supposedly unrelated items on his mind: 1) his daughter moving out of state; 2) preparing for retirement; and 3) going through a divorce. What might be a common thread?

We identified loss (abandonment) as the theme or common thread, therefore, he felt understood and great relief before having to get into any specifics. If any one of the three items had been addressed separately, it would have been a disservice to Alex and his well-being since all of them are relevant and tied to a theme. Coaching Alex was also a matter of discerning what was and what was not in his control.

Awareness of themes transforms the way you develop coaching questions and helps create transformational shifts (versus transactional) for your client. You get to the essence of what they're conveying in an efficient and effective way. As you read the rest of this chapter, don't try to commit each theme to memory; just take them in and start to make connections between coaching conversations and some of the themes that have shown up. Over time, you'll find it easier to recognize the themes at play.

The list below divides twenty-five themes into four categories: Valuable Insights, Personal Empowerment, Creating Connections, and Eliminating Obstacles. Each group contains themes that exemplify the category and all themes are covered in detail.

Common Themes in Coaching©

Valuable Insights
Ambivalence
Attached to the Outcome
Carrying Old Messages
Either/Or
Expectations
Wherever you go, there you are

Personal Empowerment
Authenticity
Hardware Store for Milk
Permission
Taking It Personally
Unmet Needs
Wanting things to be different from what is

Creating Connections
Abandonment
Alienation
Authority / Victim
Boundaries
Caretaking/ People-Pleasing
Lone Wolf

Eliminating Obstacles
Ignoring Intuition
Not in the Present
Perfection and Control
Stuck in a Strategy
Tunnel Vision

As you read through the different themes, consider how recognizing them as they arise can inform your question, and how helpful they can be when you are aiming to remain in the "helicopter" and out of the details. For each theme, I include a coaching approach when engaging with your client.

SELF-ESTEEM — THE ROOT OF ALL THEMES

To hate others is ugly. To hate yourself is uglier.
— Hlovate

Before getting into the themes on the chart, let's explore the theme that underlies all of them — self-esteem.

The bottom layer of almost all our clients' challenges is a degree of diminished self-worth. The struggle or conflict is a symptom. Underlying every theme is the issue of self-esteem or how we view ourselves. No matter the nuances and details of the situation a client is experiencing — from a relationship conflict to striving for a promotion or setting clear boundaries — the root of the challenge seems to be consistently predicated on self-esteem.

We typically don't address self-esteem head on in coaching, though enhancing self-esteem is often a by-product. As we help a person feel empowered, make better choices, understand themselves better, address their needs, and live from their values, we are helping them build self-esteem.

> *There are many variations of behaviors based on the belief that deep down we are not good enough. It's human nature to wear "masks" and build layers that conceal who we really are instead of remembering that we are the jewel inside.*

The following behaviors describe insufficient self-esteem. When you hear any of these behaviors, it's very likely your client has a self-esteem theme.

- **They believe they don't deserve or are not good enough.**
  They wind up believing the "inner voice" — the one that keeps telling them, "You aren't good enough"; "You don't know enough"; "That's for other people, not for you"; "You couldn't possibly succeed at that"; "You have no luck — don't even bother trying."
  A corresponding metaphor: It seems like everyone else has gone to the party while you've chosen to stay home wishing you had gone.

- **They overcompensate.**
  They take excessive measures, attempting to correct or make amends for an error, weakness, or problem. For example,

one parent believes the other is too strict or too lenient and goes too far the other way to make up for it.

- **They do things for other people to make themselves feel better.**
  While it's always nice to do things for other people, sometimes the motive is wanting to feel better about oneself versus simply helping someone else.

- **They compromise on things they shouldn't.**
  They might let go of or give up on an idea or value to please someone else.

- **They get into or stay in toxic relationships.**
  Relationships — whether with those at work, with friends, or with romantic partners — can be damaging to our self-esteem. Yet because they devalue themselves, they rationalize and justify that it's okay.

- **They tolerate unacceptable behavior.**
  Because they believe they aren't good enough, they allow people to say and do mean or inappropriate things to them. When they stay stuck in the way they allow others to take advantage of them, it's usually because there's a subtle, underlying reason they want to keep the pain and anguish with them. They might think that they will get attention or feel important, or maybe feeling sorry or sad is more familiar and comfortable. They don't believe they deserve to be treated well.

- **They don't set and hold good boundaries to protect themselves.**
  They don't set limits on what is and what is not acceptable for other people to do to them. And, if and when they do set limits, they back down and allow the behavior to continue.

- **They don't ask for what they want.**
  Because they believe they don't deserve good things or a better life, they don't ask for them.

- **They berate themselves.**

  They beat themselves up more than anyone else because they feel as though they have failed in some way, even if it was a simple, honest mistake. And they stay quiet about it for fear of being wrong or sounding stupid.

- **They seek perfection in themselves and/or others.**

  When they can't be perfect, they give themselves a hard time instead of accepting what is. Or, they look for other people's faults to make them feel better rather than looking at themselves, which is only a temporary fix.

- **They focus on the negatives.**

  They believe that everyone else's life is better or more important than theirs. Instead of looking at all the good things they have, they compare their lives to those of others. One tiny negative comment can linger forever in their memory while all the compliments and praise go unnoticed.

- **They tend to stay quiet and suffer.**

  At times it makes sense to speak up and say what is wanted, but they hold back because they see themselves as not worthy or deserving.

- **They don't acknowledge the beauty and gifts they bring to the world.**

  Instead, they dismiss as negligible or immaterial that which they offer to the world.

One thing to remember: it's not always appropriate to mention the theme to your client. Saying something like "I see you have a self-esteem theme going on" is obtuse and insensitive. But depending on the openness of your client and their theme, it could make sense to name it and share it, because it could answer their questions as to why their behavior hasn't been supporting what they want.

Coaching Approach

In each of the above examples, we can point out what we observe and question it. As an example, Penelope complains about wanting more time with her husband but doesn't discuss that desire with her husband. You get a sense that she doesn't believe she deserves to get what she wants and chooses to stay silent. You can point out the dynamic and ask a question such as, "What is keeping you from asking for what you want?"

VALUABLE INSIGHTS

Each of the themes in this category help people to become more aware of their behaviors and thinking thus allowing them to move forward.

Ambivalence

> *When you make a choice, you change the future.*
> — Deepak Chopra

This theme shows up when someone can't make up their mind or make a decision because they're getting lost in the pros and cons.

"Well, if I do it this way, I'm going to lose that. But if I do that, I'll miss this." They're continually trying to figure out which way to go and what decision to make.

Ambivalence shows up in the most mundane ways, such as deciding between two meals from a menu. But it also shows up in significant ways, such as choosing between two careers. Even though someone feels as though they're going to be losing or missing something by making one choice versus another, it's likely not the case.

The only loss is in the constant struggle of "Should I or shouldn't I?"; "What color should I get?"; "Which one should I vote for?" It's their time and energy that is lost. There is constantly a state of confusion and uncertainty. Ambivalent people get caught up in deciding.

The problem with this theme is your client's underlying fear of what they assume will happen if they make the "wrong" decision.

* * *

Whenever Elaine goes shopping, she can't decide what to purchase. She brings home the same sweater in red and in blue, or a red sweater in two different sizes, and has trouble making a decision as to which one to keep. Eventually, she must return one or both. She spends much of her time in confusion and uncertainty. She often feels a lot of regret and has a constant feeling of being stuck.

* * *

Sam planned a trip to visit a friend in another country. He procrastinated because he wasn't able to pin down exactly when to take the week off from work. He thought airfare prices might drop if he waited. Even though that turned out to be true, by the time he had made his decision and asked for that week off, it was too late. Sam wasted lots of time, and in the end suffered the consequences.

Coaching Approach

When coaching a client who expresses ambivalence, consider questions that help the client see potential consequences of procrastinating such as "What might you miss by not making a decision?"; "What are some potential consequences of not deciding?"; "What would help you decide?"; "What if there is no wrong decision?"; "What stops you from making a decision?" When people operate out of ambivalence, painting the picture of one option in detail including pros and cons is particularly helpful. (Details in "Advanced Techniques" in Chapter 13.)

Attached to the Outcome and Expectations

We must be willing to let go of the life we planned
so as to have the life that is waiting for us.
— Joseph Campbell

Expectations set us up to believe we are in control of how something will turn out! In reality, we have no control beyond what happens in the present. The sooner we can help our clients realize that things don't always go according to plan, the sooner they can reduce their stress, discomfort, anger, and anxiety.

Being attached to the outcome shows up when someone wants, hopes, and believes that their intended, specific outcome will be achieved. Unfortunately, that is often not the case.

Our underlying fear is that our expectations will not be met, thus setting us up for disappointment. We mask our fear by planning every detail and trying to stay in control instead of accepting what happens and learning from it.

However, those expectations are totally made up. We create ideas and stories about how wonderful or awful something might be, but it hasn't taken place yet, so we can't possibly know how it will turn out. All the while, the idea of good or bad has been established even though the event hasn't yet taken place.

How many times have you planned and imagined how things would go and then something interrupted the plan? Typical challenges that bring a client disappointment or surprise include:

- They realize they aren't really passionate about their career and want to make a change.
- They love what they do but go to work one day only to find out they're being laid off.
- After being married for several years, they realize it's not what they hoped it would be.

When your client is attached to an outcome, they miss the "journey," or what's in the present. A metaphor for this theme might be a person who is constantly thinking about what's at the top of the mountain they are climbing, and therefore doesn't enjoy the beautiful scenery along the way.

Neil planned to move to another city and find a suitable job right after finishing college. However, immediately after graduating, he became seriously ill and his best-laid plans had to be put on hold. He imagined that they would never happen. His coach helped him understand that he should accept his situation and make the best of the present time before hopefully resuming his plans.

When plans fail or get altered by circumstance, we feel disappointed and disillusioned. We can react by blaming others, feeling fearful, or becoming angry that things didn't work out. However, plans are intentions rather than guaranteed outcomes.

Coaching Approach

By definition, expectations are assumptions — something hoped for in the mind. Asking questions such as, "What is true right now?" can be helpful in any situation in which your client is letting their thoughts or expectations get in the way of their current reality.

Or a question such as, "What is it costing you to keep hoping for [expectation] when it may or may not happen?" A metaphor that might be helpful: It's like a little girl who lives in an apartment in the city and has her heart set on getting a pony for her birthday.

Carrying Old Messages

No one is in your mind — you are its only driver.
— Unknown

We often hear stories about adults still buying into childhood messages received from a parent, teacher, guidance counselor, etc. As children, we take negative messages about ourselves personally and accept them as the truth, believing there is something wrong with us. Unfortunately, many of us carry them into our adult lives (sometimes subconsciously) and still believe them as adults. It's ironic that the people who made the comments have moved on with their lives while we're still allowing the comments to affect us.

* * *

Lisa was working as an entrepreneur running a fairly successful business. She often became fed up with her clients' attitudes and would blow off meetings or not return phone calls promptly. I pointed out that it seemed as though she was self-sabotaging her business and putting it in jeopardy. I asked an unusual question: "Who would be upset if you were truly successful?" Her first response was the typical, "Nobody — everyone wants me to succeed."

Upon further investigation, Lisa remembered her mother's belief that women should not go into careers but rather stay home and take care of the family. That message was still playing in her subconscious, and somewhere deep down, she believed it. Through further discussion, she discovered the message had no truth or value and was able to let it go and see it as her mother's belief. She changed her attitude and made her business a true success.

Coaching Approach

Messages like the ones Lisa received are reflections of something going on with someone else, and we don't have to buy into them. We might encounter comments that disturb us, but as adults we can consider the source and realize that the other person's fear, anger, insecurity, etc. do not have to impact how we feel about ourselves or what decisions we make. Carrying old messages is like carrying a backpack full of useless rocks.

Ultimately, helping a client realize that an old message is a belief that was pertinent to the person the message came from likely isn't pertinent to the client's life. This can create awareness. We can offer questions that present alternative perspectives such as, "What is true about that message now?" or "What do you get out of holding onto that message?" Additionally, we can share a greater truth by asking, "As a child, you didn't have choices, but now as an adult, you do. What are some possibilities you can choose now that would serve you?"

Either/Or (Black-and-White Thinking)

You always have a choice.
— Harvey Specter

When you hear "either/or," it's time to sit up and take notice. That's a signal that something is missing.

We've become accustomed to thinking that things are either strict or lenient, easy or hard, empty or full, and, more recently in the USA, red states or blue states. In every instance, there is something else that's not being considered. People tend to believe that "one way or the other" is their only option.

* * *

Paul is a teacher and was asked by four different friends if he would take care of their pets while they went on vacation. Loving the idea of some extra money, he was weighing the idea of giving up his summer freedom and accepting all of his friends' requests or saying no to all of them and enjoying the summer free and clear. What he hadn't considered was accepting only one or two of these job offers and turning the others down. That way he could get some extra cash but not feel as though he had entirely given up his summer freedom.

We get stuck in "all or nothing thinking," or believe there are no alternatives.

* * *

Joel was toying with the idea of expanding a program he offered. His thinking revolved around the idea that he would either expand it on his own or develop it with a colleague. His concerns were about the viability of working with a colleague rather than about the expansion itself. It wasn't until he was coached and shared his dilemma that he came up with the idea of creating a mini-series to test the feasibility of working with someone else and then consider the possibility of expanding the program.

Coaching Approach

When you hear your client using black-and-white thinking, ask questions to open their thinking and help them find additional options. It can often be a matter of combining two options; other times it can be another option that had not occurred to them. While your client might not like the alternatives, it's important that they know they exist so they are making a conscious choice.

Wherever You Go, There You Are

You wander from room to room
Hunting for the diamond necklace
That is already around your neck.
— Rumi

This theme is named after Jon Kabat-Zinn's book about mindfulness, *Wherever You Go, There You Are*. People tend to think they can fix their problems by focusing outward. They believe that changing their environment will change their problem. Instead, they need to look at themselves and take responsibility for what they are or are not doing.

* * *

113

Martin shared that he wanted to move to another country because that way, "I have a better chance of meeting someone special." In truth, he could meet someone special anywhere. What would stay the same, even if he moved, was *him* — his problem was going to go with him. Martin hadn't realized that perhaps he was doing something to sabotage his chances of having a satisfying relationship right where he was.

When we don't get a promotion, make the team, or get another date, the tendency is to go to a different company, try a different team, or "move to a different country," only to discover that the same thing occurs again. We want to blame someone or something external instead of accepting that we are the common denominator and possibly the main reason for not getting what we want. Instead of blaming, we need to first face the reality of our part in the perceived problem.

Coaching Approach

It is helpful to point out that no matter what change the client believes will "fix" their problem, they are still the common denominator. Sharing the expression "If you keep on doing what you've always done, you will keep getting what you've always gotten" can be useful followed by a question asking for their thoughts about this.

PERSONAL EMPOWERMENT

The following themes relate to empowering people to feel liberated and unburdened.

Authenticity

> *The final freedom is choosing to live who you are —*
> *especially when it's scary, uncertain,*
> *inconvenient, or unpopular.*
> — Kim George

Authenticity is about knowing who we really are and what we really want. We usually know what we don't want, but we tend not to think about what we do want and what is important to us.

People who live authentic lives are able to embrace their vulnerability and know that what they do is not connected to their self-worth. This allows them to be open and honest and not fear consequences.

According to professor and author Brené Brown, people who believe "I am enough" are authentic. Unfortunately, your clients often choose "I will stay safe" instead of believing they are "enough" and living authentically.

* * *

Renata was hoping to make a decision between staying in yet another unsatisfying job or changing her career to her long-time passion of screenwriting (her major in college). Because of her fear that she couldn't succeed as a screenwriter, she continually "played it safe" and stayed in unsatisfying jobs. Through coaching, she realized that she could pursue screenwriting, which felt authentic and true, while still working in her job to reduce risk.

Coaching Approach

When you notice that your client isn't living authentically and is living someone else's vision or making choices that don't align with their values, it's important to share your observation: "It seems as though this isn't what you really want. What's true about that?" Alternatively, a useful question could be, "What would you do differently if you lived every day without fear of the outcome?" or "What would your life be like if you stepped outside of your comfort zone?"

Going to the Hardware Store for Milk

You cannot hang out with negative people and expect to live a positive life.
— Joel Osteen

One of my favorite expressions, that I first heard from Cheryl Richardson, *New York Times* best-selling author and lifestyle-makeover coach on *The Oprah Winfrey Show*, is "What has you going to the hardware store for milk?"

We naturally have expectations of other people. We want them to do something, act in a particular way, give us something, or provide something we need. Unfortunately, there are times when the person we want something from is just not capable of giving it. We get annoyed and frustrated, when in actuality we haven't chosen the appropriate person to meet the particular need.

For example, if we get upset and distressed and seek a good listener to offer sympathy and compassion, we might choose a person who is cold and aloof, setting ourselves up for disappointment. It's more than likely that there's someone more appropriate who would naturally meet our need.

* * *

Allie, a recent college graduate, was living with two male roommates. One of the guys seemed to have more in common with her socially. Because she was new to the area, she wanted to be friends with him and meet others through him. But she kept finding herself frustrated because he kept doing things that irked her.

She consistently told stories about this guy not following through, leaving the kitchen in a mess, not contributing to the household appropriately, and not always including her when he had promised to do so. There seemed to be a disconnect between the continuous complaints and her strong desire to be good friends with him.

Then I asked her, "What has you going to the hardware store for milk?" I was pointing out that this particular person was demonstrating behavior contrary to what she needed, and that he wasn't capable of meeting her expectations.

Jacob complained that the only time he received feedback from his boss was when it was negative. He spoke with his boss and expressed his desire to receive not only constructive feedback but also affirmative or positive feedback. He approached him a few times with this request, but nothing really changed. The question "What has you going to the hardware store for milk?" helped open Jacob's mind to the realization that this particular boss wasn't capable of or willing to change.

Coaching Approach

When your client is seeking support from the wrong person, point this out and help them see there might be other people or resources that can give them what they want. This is a time when naming the theme, "This sounds like going to the hardware store and expecting to get milk," resonates with clients.

Permission

> *Remember: the only person's permission*
> *you need to live your dreams is your own.*
> — Mastin Kipp

Almost every coaching conversation involves permission in some way. Either you as the coach inherently have or need permission to share something and/or you want to give your client permission to proceed in some way.

Many of our choices and decisions are based on giving or getting permission. Feeling the need to get permission often stems from feeling that we don't inherently deserve to do something (the self-esteem theme) or deserve to do it in a particular way. We're fraught with trepidation, guilt, shame, or fear of how we will be perceived. Consider sharing a metaphor such as: "This is like a person who wants to enroll in graduate school but waits for six people to say it's okay." Alternatively, for a client who often uses metaphors, ask your client to create their own metaphor by asking, "If you could imagine a picture of what this need for permission might look like, what would you see?"

Coaching Approach

When this is the case, you can help your client realize that their fear of disappointment or judgment might not be relevant or realistic. If they state, "I just want you to give me permission," you might respond, "It seems as though this is about giving yourself permission. What difference would it make if I give you permission?"

Depending on the coaching conversation, you can grant the permission: "It seems sensible to take the day off and sleep in if that will help you recover. What would that be like?" However, most often your focus should be on getting your client to give themselves permission, allowing them to discuss their impending decision, and asking what it is they would really love to do if there were no consequences. That usually helps them realize that it makes sense to go ahead. The result is that they grant their own permission, a far more empowered position for them.

Taking It Personally

Someone can intentionally send emotional poison, and if you don't take it personally, you will not eat it. When you don't take the emotional poison, it becomes even worse in the sender, but not in you.
— Don Miguel Ruiz

From the familiar "I guess I wasn't qualified for the job" to "What have I done wrong?" we consistently wonder how we could have done things differently. "How come after I told someone a better way, they chose to ignore my great advice?" It's almost inevitable that whatever happens (good or bad), we want to believe that what's going on is all about us. While it *feels* as though it's about us — it's actually not. We might be the trigger or the object, but in truth it's about the person who holds the feeling.

You'll encounter the theme of taking it personally regularly in your coaching conversations (and in your own life).

* * *

One of my single clients, Lindsey, told me about a guy she met at a party. She was excited because they had some really great discussions and a good connection. At the end of the evening, she asked him if he would like to meet again. He said he wasn't interested. Somewhat surprised and dismayed, she left the party feeling dejected and wondering, "Was it something I said? Perhaps he wasn't attracted to me?" Several days later when talking with a friend, Lindsey found out that the guy is gay and clearly would not have been interested in pursuing a romantic relationship with her.

When a situation doesn't go our way, it's not because there's something "wrong" with us; it can be as simple as our not meeting the need that was sought.

* * *

Larry didn't get a specific job he wanted. His first thoughts were, "I'm not qualified" and "I messed up on the interview." We discovered that the company wanted to hire a mature, assertive female who could deal with the difficult manager of the department. As a young male, Larry had no chance for that particular spot no matter how great his resume and interview.

Coaching Approach

By taking things personally and going straight to, "What did I do?" or "Why didn't they take my advice?" we create undue distress. But no matter what we have or haven't done, the other person has explicit needs that we might not be aware of. Pointing out this concept to your client can be liberating in that they no longer need to blame or berate themselves but can instead realize that the other person is "holding the poison" and they don't have to eat it. A question such as, "What if Bob gets triggered when anyone speaks to him during his lunch as you encountered, what would that mean for you?"

A metaphor for taking it personally: Believing it rained specifically to ruin your outdoor party.

What others say and do is a projection of their
own reality, their own dream. When we really see people
as they are without taking it personally,
we can never be hurt by what they say or do.
— Don Miguel Ruiz

Unmet Needs

It's never overreacting to ask for what you want and need.
— Amy Poehler

Get your personal needs met, once and for all;
if you have unmet needs, you'll attract others in the same position.
— Thomas J. Leonard

When a child has a temper tantrum or cries for no apparent reason, it's fairly obvious that there's something they want or need. Because they can't articulate this, they act out in a dramatic way. It's ironic that adults often behave in a similar fashion, although more subtly.

When adults aren't getting their deep, underlying needs met, or harbor unexpressed emotion, they can unconsciously behave in ways that are unhealthy. They are typically not aware of the underlying emotion or need that is not being fully met. Their negative behavior is triggered by an unconscious need not being met and could repel others.

* * *

Sierra was upset that her friend hadn't given her explicit information that she felt should have been shared. Instead of realizing and acknowledging that she was angry or hurt by this omission, Sierra became curt and

120

unaccommodating, not realizing that she was feeling a lot more than anger. She didn't know how bothered she was until her negative behavior showed up. We discovered that she was feeling undervalued — as if she wasn't important enough to have received the information. Had Sierra been able to figure out the underlying, unfilled need (feeling valued) and then expressed it, a mature conversation may have ensued.

A classic example of a subtle need is the client's urge to be complimented. They do everything they can so you will say something nice. Their underlying need may be for praise, admiration, approval, or recognition to fulfill their desire to feel worthy. Once they become aware of their unfulfilled need, they no longer need to fish for compliments; they can ask trusted friends to fulfill the need at opportune times, and/or they can surround themselves with people who support them and naturally fulfill that need.

* * *

Joanne was frustrated and annoyed after having a conversation with her supervisor. She described the interaction as one-sided. She said that her supervisor seemed to ignore and avoid her questions. I pointed out that it seemed as though she wasn't feeling heard, and I questioned what that was like for her. She agreed and said that she appreciates being heard, so I asked, "Where else in your life do you not feel heard?" which opened up a deeper coaching conversation.

In reverse, when a client notices someone's unmet need through that person's behavior, they might decide to be the one who helps fulfill it.

* * *

Christina was complaining bitterly about her new friend and how demanding she was. When I asked her, "What do you think her greatest need might be?" she responded, "Being in charge." I then asked, "If that's what she needs, what might be some occasions when you could support her being in charge?" She said, "I can let her choose the restaurant after deciding on the type of food we want." Over the next few weeks of encouraging her friend to take charge of this and several other simple choices, Christina noticed a dramatic difference in their rapport.

Coaching Approach

The good news about recognizing underlying and unfulfilled needs is that you can help your client find healthy, positive ways to have them met. It starts with noticing your client's behavior and asking yourself, "Exactly what is it they really need?" When Robin complained about her boss consistently glossing over what she contributes in meetings, it seemed as though the underlying need was to be recognized, acknowledged, or appreciated. A helpful question could be, "What do you need from your boss?" When the need is identified, the client can express it, discuss it, and learn how to ask for it. Frequently, the unmet need stems from childhood.

When there's an unmet need, the resulting behavior can be subtle — putting someone down, acting snippy, manipulating, wisecracking, withdrawing, etc. When you notice your client has an unmet need such as control, safety, worthiness, acceptance, approval, being heard, being right, being recognized, being praised, getting attention, etc., point it out and help them create healthy ways to get their need met.

Note that unmet needs are deeper than values. They are inherent from the time we are very young — they have always been there. Values, on the other hand, are developed and change over time based on our self-awareness as we mature. For example, if compassion is a guiding force in your life, it likely developed through experiences in adulthood and therefore, is a value.

The key to distinguishing a need from a value is if it was present as a young child, it is likely a need. If it developed over time, it is likely a value (such as peace, integrity, or efficiency).

That said, some ideas are both needs and values, but for different reasons. When someone was a young child, a parent often fabricated lies to cover up an addiction. Therefore, the need for honesty was deeply rooted. For someone else, they had a series of unhealthy relationships as an adult and therefore value honesty.

Wanting Things to Be Different from What Is

The amount a person suffers in their life is directly related to how much they are resisting the fact that things are the way they are. This has got to be one of the key pieces of wisdom about being human. If there is suffering or discomfort, there is resistance to the way things are.
— *Bill Harris*

When someone wants something to be different from what is, that's when suffering occurs. It is in letting go of the desire for something different and accepting the current state that the suffering can end. This does not imply giving up and surrendering. It applies when a person wants something to be different, but the circumstances don't support their desire.

* * *

Debra complained constantly about her aging parents and how much time and energy they required, and often mentioned how much she wanted her siblings to share the responsibilities even though they had no interest in doing so.

Coaching Approach

If you point out that circumstances are what they are, your client can choose to make a change or accept them. While neither may be palatable, living with what is true can allow them to realize that accepting circumstances and letting go of the idea that things

123

should be different will end the suffering. It is also helpful to ask what it's costing to hold on to wanting things to be different when they can't be so.

CREATING CONNECTIONS

The following themes involve how people connect (and disconnect) from other people. Most people have a strong need for community and connection but often behaviors sabotage connecting in a meaningful way.

Abandonment

> *If you realize that all things change, there is nothing you will try to hold on to.*
> — Lao Tzu

This theme is about dreading loss. Typically, it is about losing someone or something (job). Generally, this is a person who is not going to take a lot of risk. The thought of leaving is just as painful as the idea of being left behind. The same emotions are triggered either way. They get attached to this thought pattern instead of realizing that nothing is permanent. And they become attached to non-permanent things, so loss is inevitable.

When someone has experienced a deep loss or serious trauma, it often establishes a pattern in their thinking (not necessarily on a conscious level) that as life unfolds, the loss or trauma will recur. It's natural to feel angry, disappointed, or sad when a relationship ends, but for some people the loss is far more devastating because it triggers feelings from an earlier loss.

It's not uncommon for people with a fear of abandonment to remain in negative situations, relationships, or jobs or to hold on to possessions far too long.

* * *

Vincent lost his mother when he was very young. Now he stays in a relationship with a wife who treats him poorly.

He's not happy in the marriage, but the idea of divorce triggers feelings of loss, so he does his best to ignore his wife's verbal abuse and passive-aggressive actions.

Through coaching, when he became aware of how losing his mother and the fear of leaving was interfering with his happiness as an adult, Vincent finally was able to leave his marriage and move forward.

* * *

Gregory shared that he was afraid to leave his job even though he knew it wasn't a great fit. His fear was that he wouldn't find another one with equal compensation, so he overstayed and became really burned out. It was all about staying in his misery and not letting go of the perceived fear.

In coaching, he became aware that he hadn't even explored other opportunities. Once he recognized that and began looking at other jobs, he was amazed to discover that the potential possibilities were far greater than he had imagined. He realized that he wouldn't be losing as much as he anticipated by leaving. Rather, he had much to gain.

Coaching Approach

In coaching it's appropriate to help your client become aware that letting go of their pain almost always outweighs the perceived loss. For some clients, however, the risk of letting go feels worse than the misery they're enduring. It's important to help them see the value in choosing to let go of their pain so they can move forward.

When there's a lost relationship involved, your client might not see any possible gains or silver lining in their future if they leave the relationship. Helping them imagine unexpected possibilities may contribute to them letting go.

As human beings, we attach a certainty to ideas and people and take them for granted. Yet, in reflection, we often see that our lives are better because we have let go of the past and become open to future possibilities that prove to be greater than anticipated.

Alienation

> *We sometimes think we want to disappear,*
> *but all we really want is to be found.*
> — Unknown

This theme is about isolation and separation. It can manifest in one of two ways: the feeling of inferiority and the feeling of superiority. Either way, people feel they are different and separate from others. They typically feel a lack of fulfillment, and even mistrust.

The person who believes they are inferior is afraid of joining a group or team for fear of rejection. Accordingly, rather than taking the chance of feeling rejected, they reject themselves by not even attempting to join.

On the flip side, the person who believes they are superior doesn't need a group or team and isolates themselves. In their mind, they are "better than" or "already know." They might join a group only if they can be the leader. Ironically, this usually backfires, and they come across as a bossy know-it-all and end up alienated and alone.

* * *

Bradley always ate lunch by himself at work. Despite wanting to feel more connected, he continually rejected offers from co-workers to join them. He felt as though they were a tight-knit group and were just being polite. I asked, "What would it be like if you could join them?" He shared that it would make him happy and feel more a part of his team. After asking him, "What if the invitation is truly genuine — what would that mean for you?" he shared that he would gladly accept. After pointing out that he was already unhappy eating by himself, I asked what would happen if he took the chance and joined them, and consequently he realized that the invitation was genuine. This opened up a possibility in his mind that allowed him to take that risk instead of remaining in the unhappiness he was experiencing.

Coaching Approach

Helping a client recognize how miserable they are because they feel they don't belong, or aren't part of a group or team, is a starting place. It's often the fear of rejection, so it's useful to point out how unhappy they are and that they are rejecting themselves before giving a fair chance for connection.

Authority and Victim

Every person has free choice. Free to obey or disobey the Natural Laws. Your choice determines the consequences. Nobody ever did, or ever will, escape the consequences of his choices.
— Alfred A. Montapert

Some of us embrace and welcome rules; they create a feeling of safety and order. For others, they are annoying and sometimes ignored. They are a nuisance, feel confining, and seem irrelevant. Yet rules, by nature, are neutral.

Resistance is how it usually manifests — we refuse to do anything we're told to do, simply because we're told to do it. It's almost as if we throw our hands up and say, "Stop telling me what to do."

Control, competition, and conflict are all parts of this theme, and it involves vying for power or freedom. If someone says, "No, I really have a better way of doing this," or "I don't like doing it your way," it's a clue they're operating from this theme. They might also like to give advice and then get annoyed when others don't follow it.

What is it about rules that cause us to be submissive or rebellious?

127

To understand how the theme might show up, imagine that Betsy and Joe were flying on an airplane. Both preferred aisle seats but were assigned middle seats, and after takeoff, the aisle seats next to them remained empty. Betsy felt compelled to remain in the middle seat because that was her assigned seat. Joe, on the other hand, immediately occupied the empty seat.

What's incongruous about this theme is that just as we want to wield power and control, at other times we succumb to feeling like a victim of authority. It's ironic that someone who can be authoritative can also feel like a victim — helpless, powerless, and as though they have no choice or authority. Therefore, the two themes are interrelated. Either way, their fate is determined by someone or something else. It manifests as "Poor me. I have no choice [no power; no authority] to do anything about it."

> *We may succumb to powerlessness, helplessness, and victimization,*
> *but then we swing to the other extreme by aggressively*
> *wielding power over those around us.*
> — Melodie Beattie

* * *

Sandra told me how much she disliked her boss because she told her exactly how she wanted things done and Sandra didn't necessarily agree. When I inquired if it would have made a difference if her boss had suggested how something could be done rather than insisting on how to do it, she explained that given a choice she might have felt more open to her boss's way of doing it. In essence, Sandra automatically rebelled against what seemed to her like a rule. She wasn't opposed in principle; she was opposed to what felt like a demand.

Coaching Approach

Whether a client buys into or dismisses the rules, they act as if they have no choice. You ultimately want to help them be proactive and have a say in how things occur and turn out. Empowerment comes from mastering the middle ground and discerning in each instance whether the rule or directive is valid. You want to help them look at each situation and choose accordingly rather than submit to or reject the rules automatically.

How a message is delivered is frequently confused with the content of the message. You want to help your client separate *how* something is requested from *what* is requested. For those who typically oppose rules, this can dramatically shift the result from reacting automatically to making a powerful choice. Separating the message from the delivery or standing on principle is like turning down a front row concert ticket because you don't like the person who is offering it.

When you hear a client lamenting as though they have no choice (no power), it is helpful to point out that we *always* have a choice, and we have the power to make the choice. In some situations, a question such as, "What is allowing you to give more power to [the other person]?" helps to create the awareness that it's simply an idea rather than truth.

Believing you don't have choices is the most common limiting belief.
— Arthur Basley

Boundaries

You teach people how to treat you by what you allow,
what you stop, and what you reinforce.
— T. Gaskins

After self-esteem, the most common theme is related to boundaries. When was the last time someone:

- Asked you to do something that you didn't have the time or desire to do, but you felt compelled to say yes anyway?
- Said something that offended you and you remained quiet?
- Stood too close and you felt uncomfortable and needed to step back?

Clients rarely come to coaching asking for help with boundaries. Rather, it comes in the form of a story describing boundaries being invaded or crossed.

What exactly is a boundary? It's a means to protect ourselves from emotional or physical harm from others. Boundaries are about other people affecting our well-being. We need to clearly know what's okay and what's not okay *for us*. No two people have exactly the same boundaries since we have different thresholds, different tolerance levels, and different values.

Healthy boundaries help us experience comfortable interdependence with other people. A person with no boundaries is unable to prevent unwanted intrusions.

Samples of setting boundaries:

- You are standing too close for my comfort.
- I will not complete it unless I get more information.
- I'm not able to pick up your groceries.
- I can't stay later than five o'clock.
- I'm uncomfortable when you touch me while we are talking.
- I'm not okay with offensive language.

It's important to note that to set a boundary is to inform. But people don't always abide by our requests. Therefore, we should be prepared to share a consequence if they continue to violate a request. For example, "If you continue to use foul language, *this conversation is over.*" Most important, we *must* follow through on the consequence. If we don't, nothing changes, and we've wasted our breath.

We are entitled to change our mind, make mistakes, say, "I don't know," ask for more time, not offer excuses, or make a decision without having to justify it. We want our clients to expand their safe space and keep bad behaviors even further away.

There are many hooks that cause us to ignore boundaries for fear of negative consequences, such as:

- If I give the relationship enough time, things will change. (It's okay to set time limits in relationships.)

- I have to think and act in ways that will preserve the relationship no matter what toll it may take. (You are not responsible for the actions of another person.)

- I'm willing to forego money, friends, and/or self-respect for the sake of my relationship. (Your personal worth is not dependent on anyone else.)

There has been an increased awareness of boundaries in the media over the last few years. Many of your clients will be aware of the term but unsure exactly how to determine their boundaries and enforce them with others. This theme can lead to rich coaching conversations.

Be aware that it is uncomfortable for many people to set and maintain boundaries. They worry about not being liked and how they will be perceived by others — that they will "get in trouble" or be perceived as cold. When first setting boundaries, they often feel guilty for speaking up for themselves and placing their needs above someone else. Ironically, they are more likely to be respected for knowing what they want/don't want.

Coaching Approach

In coaching conversations in which boundaries are the heart of the problem, it's helpful to ask the client for their definition of *boundary*. Depending on their response, I might announce taking off my coaching hat and say, "Boundaries are what's okay and what's not okay for other people to do in your presence. What does that mean for you?" Just hearing that definition can create awareness in the client.

Ask questions that help your client discover what their preferred boundaries are in various situations. An easy way to do this is to ask them to think of a time when they felt resentful or uncomfortable as that will likely describe when a boundary was violated. Then have them devise ways to inform others of those boundaries and follow through with consequences when their boundaries are not respected.

Developing, articulating, and enforcing healthy boundaries is a long-term process that requires practice. You won't be able to help your client solve this challenge in a single session! However, attention to this theme will have long-lasting, positive results.

Caretaking and People-Pleasing

When you try to please everybody, you end up pleasing nobody because you spread it too thin.
— Norman Levine

When we hear the word *abundance*, we typically think of plentiful and bountiful. When someone feels secure and confident about who they are and what they have, they can give freely without needing or wanting anything in return. We often think of philanthropists as generous people who give freely because they have more than enough money for themselves.

We can also see it in people who don't have much of their own yet have no problem giving to others because they find it spiritually uplifting.

* * *

Diana, a graphic designer, was struggling to start a freelance business. When she met another business owner at a networking meeting, she thought it was a shame that he had such a great business name, but his business card didn't reflect that at all. So Diana designed an incredible card and logo and sent it to the business owner with no return address and no identifying information.

On the other hand, someone might give generously while being unaware that they hope to get something in return. Abundance and people-pleasing are intertwined based on giving.

* * *

Louise decided to purchase a van so she could transport people who didn't have their own transportation. She offered to pick them up and take them to their weekly meetings and appointments. When people did not express appreciation, she complained that people were taking advantage of her.

We may subliminally expect something in return — gratitude, recognition, or payment — for helping others. When that doesn't happen, we feel resentment: "Why am I going out of my way to help people and they won't even say thank you?" This demonstrates that we have an ulterior motive for being generous even though it appears to be coming from abundance.

This shows itself in the form of people-pleasing. It is often present in a person who loves to give advice, believing they are really helping people. When the advice is not followed, they become frustrated, and while they believed they were giving the advice from a feeling of abundance, it was more likely from a desire to control the other person.

When you hear your client lamenting, "I've been doing so much and I'm not getting anything," and you can see that the resentment has been quietly building, then you know it's not abundance; it's people-pleasing — putting everyone else's needs before their own and not taking time to examine their needs or what's best for them.

Because people-pleasers have a propensity to care about everyone else's well-being except their own, they do more and give more than they receive for fear of losing someone's love or respect. They tend to say yes to everything despite their feelings.

The following examples demonstrate how a client minimizes what they need for the sake of pleasing other people. It's your role to help them see that their giving is motivated by an underlying need to be liked, loved, needed, included, or accepted, and that they can have these things without giving so much. If not, the person who is taking advantage of them likely shouldn't be a part of their life. In fact, they might gain the person's respect by saying no to things that don't suit them.

* * *

Wendy told a story about her mother being abusive and nasty. Yet she wanted her mother's love so desperately that she was willing to put up with awful, unacceptable behavior just to remain in a relationship with her despite the many negative consequences.

* * *

Lucas frequently complained about his boss and co-workers placing too many demands on him. When we discussed this, he realized that he volunteered to help others although it was not required. We discussed his motivation and discovered that his need to feel needed and important was so strong that he wasn't able to see his own value without helping co-workers.

Coaching Approach

The thinking behind someone's people-pleasing is that the easiest way to feel worthwhile is to meet someone else's needs so that they will care about them, providing temporary strength and supposed control.

To break this cycle, we need to help our clients form healthy boundaries, take care of themselves without guilt, appreciate other people without losing themselves in the process, and stand up and share when a behavior is unacceptable to them.

> *We are not responsible for another person's behavior and they are not responsible for our well-being.*

Clients who can't say no usually feel overwhelmed because they have too much on their plate — or resentful because they do too much. People who put themselves last aren't aware of just how unhealthy their relationships are and the harm that is being done to themselves.

Here are some questions that can help your client realize that their people-pleasing might be unhealthy:

- What are you sacrificing to keep the relationship going?
- What is it that has you solving other people's problems instead of your own?
- What has you taking responsibility for other people?
- What stops you from saying no when you're asked to do something you don't want to do?

Lone Wolf

Refusing to ask for help when you need it is refusing someone the chance to be helpful.
— Ric Ocasek

People often think that asking for help is a sign of weakness, whereas it's actually a sign of strength. It's hard to imagine that making a request of someone or asking them to assist in any way could be a good thing. They often believe that they are the only ones who can solve their problems. This can manifest when someone complains about having to do so much of the work where they're employed until it's revealed that it's because they don't delegate and insist on doing everything themselves.

Coaching Approach

There seems to be some shame involved in asking for help, as if your client will be judged poorly. Or it creates a feeling of vulnerability, which is uncomfortable or unfamiliar. Your role is to help them realize that asking for help is a sign of strength. It proves they're human, and that there's no need to allow pride to get in the way of making something easier.

ELIMINATING OBSTACLES

Each of the themes in this category has to do with an obstacle that is keeping a person from moving forward.

Ignoring Intuition

Intuitions are not to be ignored. They represent data processed too fast for the conscious mind to comprehend.
— Sherlock Holmes

We often receive warning signs or signals and choose to ignore them or, at best, acknowledge them and still proceed as planned. Despite obvious evidence of the *Titanic* sinking, a passenger thought, "I'll keep on dancing. This ship was built to last and will never sink." Ignoring intuition can manifest as refusing to believe what we already know deep down.

* * *

After receiving a recommendation, Bruce hired someone to add new links to his website. After agreeing on a price and being reassured that it was a small job and would only take a few days, more than a week passed. When it wasn't completed within two weeks, he sent emails and called and was assured it would be completed long before his deadline. Each week, Bruce contacted the person and was assured not to worry and to be patient. As his coach, I helped him pay more attention to his "inner knowing" that the job might not happen. With the deadline approaching, Bruce finally hired another web designer who completed the job in two days.

Red flags are constantly present — revealing and pointing something out. Yet, too often people are too busy to pay attention, are relying on their intentions or impulses, or are not truly present. That's when they choose (sometimes subconsciously) to ignore the signals. It costs them time, money, and energy.

Coaching Approach

When a red flag (or warning) shows up, you can help your client become more aware of their intuition and make conscious decisions in the moment. When their "little voice" or inner knowing lets them know something is awry, they have a choice to ignore it or take action. When a client needs to make a decision and they are hemming and hawing, an observation and question that comes from your intuition such as, "It seems as though you know what you really want, what might be stopping you from making the decision?" can be useful to get to the underlying reason that is preventing action.

Not in the Present

> *The past exists only in our memories, the future only in our plans.*
> *The present is our only reality.*
> — *Robert Pirsig*

A vast majority of people live either predominantly in the past ("I wish I had...") or in the future ("What if..."). But the only time frame that matters is the present.

When something is already completed or in the past, we can't go back and change it. And when we realize that the past is part of being human, we can learn to forgive ourselves and look at how we might do things differently if a similar situation or circumstance arises again.

When I tell students that there is no past and no future, they think I've lost my mind. What this really means is that the past is over, and now the only way it can exist is in our minds. The future hasn't happened yet; that, too, can only exist in our minds and imagination, like a person on a first date planning their wedding.

"Should" stems from the ego or the outside. It is what you believe others think is correct or right for you. The word *should* often implies not being in the present but rather concerned about a past regret or a future thought. When we say or hear the word *should* in relation to the past, it implies guilt or blame, as in "I should have been more careful." It can also imply "have to" or obligation when used in regard to the future, as in "My parents really want me to become a doctor. I should do what they want even though it's not what I want."

Coaching Approach

When a client comes to you afraid to live in the present and move forward, they might subconsciously fear that they will repeat the past instead of learning from it. When they're stuck with the "what if's," you can help them see that they're fretting over something that hasn't happened and may never happen.

According to author Dr. Harriet Lerner, in *The Dance of Fear: Rising above Anxiety, Fear, and Shame to Be Your Best and Bravest Self,* "Only when we experience emotions as both potential stumbling blocks and wise guides, not either/or, can we begin to live more fully in the present and move into the future with courage, clarity, humor, and hope."

Again, asking "What is true right now?" forces your client to realize that in the present moment their thoughts are the only thing propelling their fear or regret.

Perfection and Control

> *The essence of being human is that one does not seek perfection."*
> — George Orwell

One of the hardest things to do is let someone do something their way when it doesn't match our way. Letting go of what we believe is the "right" way releases our need to control every situation, person, place, or thing.

Things you might hear a client say when perfection and/or control is the theme include:

- I can't prioritize because everything has to be perfect.
- I can't let anyone else do it.
- Nobody can do it as well as I can.
- I have to do it in a particular way, and it has to be right.

While on vacation, MaryAnn noticed that her friend chose not to change his watch to the local time. She was eager to tell him to change it, but because she was working on letting go of control, she instead kept her mouth shut when she realized that it wasn't any of her business.

* * *

Shirleen talked about her careful preparations for a dinner party. When she realized that she had forgotten to serve one of the vegetables, she gave herself a hard time. She continued dwelling on her oversight instead of simply letting it go. It was helpful for Shirleen to realize that she had no control at that point; dwelling on it only created unnecessary distress.

> *We only have control up to the point that we can do something, but we do not have control over the outcome.*

Letting clients know this can be helpful.

* * *

Roger was frustrated because he thought his project had to be done perfectly. He believed that if he monitored the project through to the bitter end, no matter how much time it took, and rechecked to make sure everything was perfect, he would be in control. But Roger was constantly exhausted. Through coaching, what he came to understand was that doing his best work was the only part in his control.

Coaching Approach

The need and desire to control is pervasive. When you hear that your client wants to control a situation or another person, your role is to help them differentiate when it's their business or concern and when it's not, and to help them realize that letting go frees up time and energy. And wanting things to be perfect only prolongs finishing something and moving on. A helpful question: "What if there is no perfect, what would that mean?"

Stuck in a Strategy

> *If you do what you've always done,*
> *you'll get what you've always gotten.*
> — Tony Robbins

One of the most interesting things about strategies is that they are so pervasive we hardly realize we're living our lives based on one or more of them. For example, someone who puts in eighty-hour work weeks to make themselves feel important.

When we participate in a group, we notice dynamics emerge. One person usually speaks first, and one person usually waits to be last. This is a strategy. Usually, we don't consciously create them. They stem from some underlying thinking process or idea. Possible reasons for creating this strategy:

- If I speak first, I will have it out of the way.
- If I speak first, I won't be called on when I don't know the answer.
- If I wait until the end, I can hear what other people say before I have to share.
- Hopefully, I will not have to share if I wait long enough [etc.].

I discuss more about strategies in Chapter 10, "Creating Shifts," because they often get in the way of what we really want; and in Chapter 15, "Advanced Coaching Techniques," I specifically address many common strategies.

Tunnel Vision

> *It is good to have an end to journey toward;*
> *but it is the journey that matters, in the end.*
> — Ernest Hemingway

While we could literally put on someone else's shoes, we cannot literally get into someone else's mind.

We get wrapped up in our own experiences, beliefs, and ideas and believe that others have the same ones. When they don't, we tend to be dismissive or intolerant rather than curious and interested. Our natural tendency is to dismiss or feel puzzled by other people's feelings and ideas when we can't identify with them. We project our feelings onto the other person. For some people a negative experience can feel traumatic, while another person shrugs it off as no big deal.

Let's begin with an example:

* * *

Anna shared a story about going swimming with her friend. It quickly became apparent that her friend was deathly afraid of water. Anna's typical response would have been, "Get over it; it's only water, and we can stay where it's shallow." But when she took the time to inquire into her friend's fear, she discovered that her friend truly believed she would drown. Anna developed an incredible amount of patience and empathy. By holding her friend's hand, and her friend holding on to the edge of the pool, Anna made it possible for her to get into the shallow end and actually relax.

When a client does or says something that you don't agree with or have not experienced, engage your curiosity. Your objective should be to understand their viewpoint or angle.

* * *

Brenda, an RN (Registered Nurse), told me about her intolerance of and lack of patience with some of the patients she cares for at the hospital. However, when she became a patient, she had major revelations. She realized that many of the challenges experienced by her patients were the same ones she complained about. This experience created a tremendous amount of empathy in Brenda and a new sense of tolerance.

Coaching Approach

When we choose to stick to our own beliefs and ideas about how something should be, our world becomes insular. We become physically or emotionally removed from others and inward-looking. When we truly "stand in someone else's shoes" and imagine where their ideas and thinking come from, only then can we minimize judgment and realize that people don't necessarily experience things the same way we do.

Learning how to stand in someone else's shoes creates a less separatist attitude in us, or, at best, a deeper connection. Our ability to do so ripples out into the world, perhaps helping someone else feel understood. Diplomacy is all about recognizing the other point of view. From that perspective, imagine how the world would be if nations were to step into other nations' shoes. It would help reduce conflict and steadfast positions and make it easier to reach compromise.

A metaphor for tunnel vision: It's as if you're drowning in a swimming pool, surrounded by swimmers, and the lifeguard is all the way at the other end of the pool but you're convinced only the lifeguard can save you.

When you're coaching someone and notice that *you* have an idea or judgment about what they're saying or how they're doing something, it's an opportunity to consider getting into *their* shoes and understanding their perspective and point of view.

USING THEMES IN COACHING

Now that you're aware of all of these themes, you have new insights into human behavior and motivation. This information has served my students, mentees, and clients in profound ways.

Whether you work as a life coach, executive coach, wellness coach, or any other type, consider learning about and listening for themes in your coaching conversations. You might not be able to identify them right from the start, but with practice you'll find them easy to recognize because they repeat over and over even though the stories behind them are different.

Themes are present in every conversation, and they are your guide to figuring out how to laser in on what matters most.

TIP: To recognize themes, listen for key phrases and statements:

- Listen for how one option prevents another option, such as "I could do X, but then I can't do Y" — Either/or.

- Notice absolute language, such as *always, never, impossible, no other choice,* etc., such as "I have to make sure it's exactly right" — Perfection and control.

- Listen for the client saying how things are beyond their control, including how there's nothing they can do to change their situation, such as "I have no choice" — Victim.

- In the Authority theme, there's usually an "I know best" accompanied by some version of blame such as, "My idea was so great, but they didn't follow it" — Authority.

- With Boundaries, listen for a sense of feeling violated or disrespected. It's about someone else doing something that is unacceptable. "He kept telling ethnic jokes that made me uncomfortable" — Boundaries.

- Simply notice if someone is unable or unwilling to make a choice, such as "Both options seem to work so I can't decide" — Ambivalence.

- When you hear beliefs related to how the grass is greener elsewhere, such as "If I move to another state, I'll find a healthy relationship" — Wherever you go, there you are.
- When the person acts like something is only happening to them and not anyone else, this is a clue that they're taking it personally. For example, "I was the only one who didn't get…" — Taking It Personally.

Now that you are aware of the themes inherent in all conversations, zeroing in on what's most important is a key to Laser-Focused Coaching. Deeper conversations lead to sustained, permanent change and impact the client's progress meaningfully.

QUESTIONS FOR REFLECTION

- What themes have you noticed in your coaching conversations?
- What difference will it make when you recognize a theme while coaching?
- What impact will identifying a theme have on your questions?
- What might be different in your coaching knowing all of the ways self-esteem can manifest?

CHAPTER 9

LASERING IN ON WHAT MATTERS MOST

Problems are like plants; you've got to get to the roots in order to prevent them from popping up again.
— Brian G. Jett

Laser-Focused Coaching is not all about asking many different questions, but rather listening for any discrepancies, underlying needs, misconceptions, or firmly held ideas that may not be true for the client. In other modalities, coaching can go in circles and take more time than necessary because there is extraneous conversation that is not productive and doesn't keep the conversation moving forward.

As you read this chapter, I invite you to recall some of your coaching sessions and consider when using Laser-Focused Coaching might have been useful.

GETTING TO THE ROOT OF THE PROBLEM

People tend to come up with strategies to handle and deal with problems. If we don't know what's causing a problem in our lives, the solutions we come up with are like putting a small bandage on a gushing wound without knowing what's causing all the gushing. They are temporary fixes. And if there's internal hemorrhaging, the bandage can hide the problem and prevent it from ever being solved.

145

Laser-Focused Coaching works because *it focuses on what created the problem before solving it.* If we don't understand where a problem comes from, the dynamic will continue into the future. In other words, if we just solve it or come up with an action plan, whatever is underneath will continue. When we move to problem-solving, we lose partnership with the client and the ability to support them to go deeper into their own learning.

SOME QUESTIONS TO HOLD IN MIND WHEN DOING LASER-FOCUSED COACHING

- What is the purpose of the story?
- What is the *emotion* they're feeling?
- What is the truth for this person?
- What does the client want the coach to hear?
- What thought does the client believe is true that may not be so?
- What is going on with the client as opposed to the other person (people) in the story?

DEEPER VERSUS BROADER

Because Laser-Focused Coaching emphasizes getting to the root of the problem, exploring under the surface of the stories, details, and descriptions gets to what's really needed to help your client.

Lasering in on a story doesn't mean summarizing and moving on to asking questions. It is about understanding where they're stuck in their thinking and what makes it a problem for them versus someone else. This includes:

- Ascertaining why your client is telling the story
- Identifying the emotion(s) they're feeling
- Checking in with them to see if the topic is really what they want to talk about or if they're just sharing something that's not relevant to what they need to work on

- Recognizing that appropriate reflection may already be considered coaching and creating awareness

STRAIGHT TO THE POINT

Rather than asking questions to get data, Laser-Focused Coaching questions distinguish truth from perception. For example, if the statement, "My boss hates me" is accepted as true, the underlying problem will not be revealed. It's critical to be skeptical of your client's perceptions because what they believe to be true might not necessarily be true.

In response to the above client's perception, asking, "How do you know your boss hates you?" is a weak coaching question because it asks for information that will merely support the perception rather than help the client move forward. That kind of question can be easier and more interesting for the coach, but it's not helpful for the client. "What is the relationship you would like to have with your boss?" is a stronger question because it moves the conversation forward and is likely something they didn't previously think about. It doesn't accept "My boss hates me" at face value.

GIVE YOUR CLIENT WHAT THEY NEED, NOT NECESSARILY WHAT THEY THINK THEY WANT

Clients often come to coaching wanting a specific outcome, solution, or result. In some other methods, coaches focus on what their client says they want and miss their deep needs. In Laser-Focused Coaching you help your client discover their true feelings and the experiences they're after and see that there are many possible ways to get to the outcome they desire.

This doesn't mean you ignore or dismiss what your client wants; it means to *listen for what's underneath their request*. More often than not there's something they need that would help them long term as opposed to giving them what they want in that moment.

147

Arthur came for coaching saying, "I want a way to figure out how I can accomplish more each day. I just don't seem to get as much work done as my counterpart in a different department."

Conventional Approach	Laser-Focused Approach
How do you know that you aren't getting as much done as your co-worker?	I get that you want to accomplish more, and I wonder what makes that important for you?
Arthur: I listen to Sue when she talks about her work and it sounds like a lot more than what I get done.	Arthur: I want to please my boss. I want him to be able to count on me to get my projects done.
What could be a way that you could get more accomplished?	What might be some differences between your projects and Sue's projects? (Arthur lists several distinctions.)
Arthur: I suppose I could...	Listening to those clear distinctions in the types of projects, what has you comparing your work to Sue's?

The bottom line is that accomplishing more was not what Arthur needed. Instead, he needed to see the value he was providing and to realize that comparison is dangerous.

I've often heard clients come to a call requesting a strategy or brainstorming that could be helpful. Although it might be tempting to brainstorm or come up with a strategy, unless we address what's underneath, it will only be a short-term solution.

* * *

Hector came for coaching and said, "For many years, I've been working as a health coach and find that I'm now getting requests for leadership coaching. I've successfully coached several leaders, but I don't feel as though I have credibility since I've never been a team leader. Perhaps we can brainstorm and come up with a strategy so that I'll feel more comfortable.

Instead of immediately believing Hector that brainstorming and strategizing would be most helpful, it quickly became evident that provocative coaching questions began to uncover what was under his insecure feelings. Some of the questions that led Hector to feeling confident about marketing himself as a leadership coach were:

- What do you need to give yourself permission to market yourself as a leadership coach?
- What is missing that would give you credibility?
- What are the qualities of a good leadership coach? (trust, integrity, etc.)
- What about you and those qualities are true right now?
- What has you thinking that health coaching and leadership coaching are so different?
- If you have already successfully coached leaders, what has you disqualifying yourself?
- What qualities about yourself would you need to acknowledge to confidently market yourself as a leadership coach?

WHEN TO USE LASER-FOCUSED COACHING

Laser-Focused Coaching does not work in every situation. It works best when your client is stuck or frustrated with an existing way of thinking and can't seem to move forward. It works well when you can identify *a limiting belief* (thought or idea), as well as one of the themes from Chapter 8, to help your client realize a different way of viewing their situation. However, not every situation is appropriate for Laser-Focused Coaching.

For example, Laser-Focused Coaching may not work well when there's an ongoing challenge such as searching for a job.

There may or may not be an underlying theme that is keeping your client from getting a job; they might just need to work on their resume or hone their interviewing skills. Yet, you want to ascertain if there's something the client believes about themselves that is preventing them from touting their accomplishments or hampering their interviewing skills. In that case, Laser-Focused Coaching makes sense.

MISTAKES TO AVOID WHEN DOING LASER-FOCUSED COACHING

- Getting too focused on the details and circumstances and forgetting the overall purpose of the story
- Trying too hard to hasten the process
- Feeling impatient and/or frustrated because you think you know the answer
- Not exploring enough about the person and jumping to conclusions
- Not getting permission or an agreement
- Not stopping when the client doesn't want to discuss a topic that you think is relevant
- Glossing over quick, seemingly insignificant comments
- Not hearing the discrepancy or disconnect
- Trying to understand the problem rather than the client
- Not getting into the client's shoes — where *they* are coming from
- Interpreting information without questioning it

Now that we've looked into understanding human behavior and discerning truth from perception, the next element of the middle portion is facilitating the client's shift in thinking.

QUESTIONS FOR REFLECTION

- What aspects of Laser-Focused Coaching seem familiar? What seems new or different?
- What does "understanding the client instead of the problem" mean to you?
- What will the awareness about greater truths mean for your coaching?
- What is your understanding of going deeper instead of broader? What impact will that have on your coaching?

CHAPTER 10

CREATING SHIFTS

A mind once stretched by a new idea never regains its original dimension.
— Oliver Wendell Holmes

There comes a time in every masterful coaching conversation when your client is ready to shift their perspective. It's a powerful moment and can be very satisfying for both you and your client. It's also a challenging moment that can cause you to struggle.

The dictionary definition of *shift* is "a change in place or position." In coaching, it's a change in perspective about a firmly held idea that may or may not be true for your client. Transformational shifts are new viewpoints that transform their thinking going forward. When your client shifts their perspective or viewpoint, new opportunities and solutions present themselves, which, in turn, create *immediate long-term change.*

All of us hold assumptions about life, and we form new untested ones every day based on how we perceive things. Our assumptions can turn client data into incorrect content. They can subtly lead us in the wrong direction versus staying on the right track. You might not realize you're assuming something, yet when you accept exactly what your client says as truth, you're assuming that it isn't perception when it might be just that. Problems occur when you accept untested assumptions as truth — either your own or your client's.

153

PARADIGM — A MODEL OF HOW WE LOOK AT THE WORLD

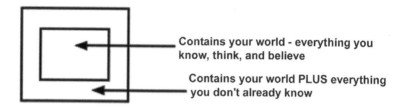

Contains your world - everything you know, think, and believe

Contains your world PLUS everything you don't already know

The smaller box in the diagram above represents your current paradigm — that is, everything you know, think, and believe — your world, so to speak. The larger box represents your world *and* everything you don't already know.

The objective in creating a shift for your client is to expand their paradigm so they become aware of things they don't already know, thus shifting their perspective. A shift results in seeing things in a new and different way that is so profound it obliterates their original way of thinking.

When a transformational shift takes place, a person's thinking is changed to such an extent that they can no longer identify with their original position. It's a mental realignment.

HOW TO INSPIRE THE DESIRE FOR "THE SHIFT"

We change our behavior when the pain of staying the same becomes greater than the pain of changing. Consequences give us the pain that motivates us to change.
— Henry Cloud

Studies show that 90 percent of people move away from pain. ("I hate my job"; "I have to get out of this relationship"; "I need to move away"; "I'm tired of scrimping.") But only 10 percent of people are motivated to move toward pleasure. ("I want to feel healthy"; "I want a fulfilling job.") Helping your client acknowledge their pain (their current situation) motivates and encourages them to move toward what they want. Unless and until you have your client's buy-in, an acceptance of just how bad things are, they likely won't be motivated enough to make a change.

LETTING GO OF PERCEIVED LIMITATIONS

All of our ideas, thoughts, values, and beliefs are subject to change, but change happens only when we receive evidence that proves there are other ways of seeing things. Our perceptions are comfortable for us, so we stick with them and usually believe they are factual and true.

There's a reason your client is holding on to an idea that prevents forward movement, otherwise they would have resolved it themselves and you wouldn't be having a coaching conversation. As a masterful coach you can help your client invent new interpretations of their perceptions and connect dots that may not be obvious to them. When they shift an interpretation that hasn't served them, new opportunities and solutions are revealed that create satisfaction and forward movement.

People devise strategies to help them get by, but many strategies, such as will power, are just *temporary measures* that don't lead to positive, permanent change. When your client becomes aware of their temporary solutions it helps them realize they aren't getting what they truly want.

* * *

Julie desperately wants to be in a fulfilling, long-lasting relationship. Her strategy is to figure out what the other person wants and work hard to meet those needs. Her strategy works temporarily because she gets into relationships, but she never gets her own deep needs met. Eventually her relationships fail, and she begins the cycle again.

Some coaches might focus on the types of men Julie chooses to date. But a more lasting shift can take place if you address her perception that she can't be herself and have her needs met in a relationship. It's important to help her realize that her strategies don't serve her.

THE MECHANICS OF A SHIFT

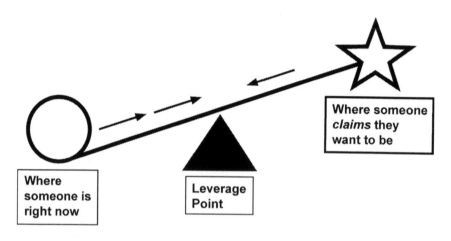

For a shift to occur, your client's thinking must be changed around their belief.

Where someone is right now

Leverage Point

Where someone *claims* they want to be

On the left side is the starting position *where the client is now* in their misery, pain, or suffering — some kind of discontent.

The mid-point between where the client is now and what they say they ultimately want is the *leverage point*. It's the point in the conversation when you hear or notice that there is a balance between where they are and the "faulty thinking" related to what they want.

On the right side is their desired change — *where they claim they want to be*. I use the word *claim* because, as much as they think that is the change they desire, it might not be aligned with their truth. Alternatively, their desire might be fraught with subconscious "faulty" ideas.

When someone is going for an outcome that is consistently not happening, it can be because *it's the wrong goal — it's not aligned with their truth.*

* * *

Alan wanted to be an entrepreneur and start a new business, but he didn't take any steps toward making it happen, and always had a different excuse for not taking those steps.

In this case, Alan came to realize that he wasn't meant to be an entrepreneur. He actually couldn't stand the idea of not having a steady income and didn't really want to tackle all the other challenges that go with being an entrepreneur. Accordingly, he had to establish a new vision that aligned with his truth.

If your client claims to want a new job, it's important to explore the reasons why and the significance of wanting the change. It might turn out that the job is not the problem, but rather it's their relationship at home (their truth).

COMPETING SUBCONSCIOUS PRIORITIES

Although it's not on a conscious level, people often self-sabotage due to unrealized competing priorities. For example, despite often committing to handing in projects on time, Bill consistently hands them in late. He isn't aware of an underlying priority: if he hands everything in on time, he will likely be promoted and deep down, he is convinced that a higher position will lead to failure. Therefore, his unrecognized priority is to stay exactly where he is. When Bill becomes aware of this conflict through coaching, he examines the underlying belief, recognizes the truth that he may just as easily succeed, and consciously chooses the priority that supports his growth.

ALIGNING WITH VISION

> *Pain will push you until the vision pulls you.*
> — Michael Bernard Beckwith

Another reason that a client doesn't move forward can be that the vision is not compelling or strong enough. If your client claims to want to go on a diet, and three weeks later they have given it up, chances are the vision wasn't compelling enough. On the other hand, if your client says, "My daughter is getting married and I want to wear this great dress I saw in a shop window, but I have to lose fifteen pounds to fit into it," chances are she's motivated and the vision is compelling enough to achieve the desired outcome.

LISTEN FOR THE LEVERAGE POINT
(Limiting Idea or Faulty Thinking)

If you're challenged to find the leverage point in the coaching process, listen for the limiting idea or faulty thinking that the client believes to be true. Everyone agrees the sky is blue, the sun sets, etc., but beliefs such as, "It's hard to get a job in a difficult economy" are not necessarily the truth for everyone.

A big part of our job is to discern what is really true and what is perception. In fact, most of what clients tell us (and most of what we tell ourselves) is perception. Your client's opinion or judgment is based on their personal filters and experiences. It might *seem* true, but if it's what's holding them back or keeping them stuck, it's your role to help them see a different perspective.

However, asking your client "What's really true here?" could be insulting because they think whatever they share is the truth. Below are some examples of how to handle this tactfully. It takes practice, and you might not be perfect at it the first time, but it will become second nature the more you try it and realize how profound it can be for your clients.

Here are some examples of the types of statements you might hear that are limiting ideas that may not be true.

- **Client**: If I share my thoughts, he will leave me. (Up till now, the client has been complaining and withholding her feelings and thoughts from her boyfriend.)

Coach: Up until now, you've been suffering in silence, so you have a choice: continue to suffer in silence or try something different and possibly get what you're hoping for. What do you want to do?

- **Client:** If I don't show up every day, the place will fall apart.
  Coach: You said that you're constantly exhausted. So you have a choice to continue being exhausted or to take a chance that the place won't fall apart in your absence. What do you want to do?

- **Client:** When my daughter goes to college, I will not survive without her.
  Coach: I've heard several complaints about your daughter's late hours, poor schoolwork, and loud music. After she leaves, what might be possible?

- **Client:** If I tell him to stop bothering me and taking advantage of my time, he will stop all referrals.
  Coach: It seems as though you have this set up in your mind as either continue to endure his advances or take a chance that if you say something he might not continue referring. What do you want to do?

Christina's story: "I love cooking and trying new recipes, but not for my husband because he is so unappreciative. I'm really stuck because I feel frustrated and resentful." As the conversation continued, the key to the leverage point was the statement "If I stop cooking for him, I will feel guilty." The coach wondered "How does she know that? That's not a fact. That's a limiting idea."

When you hear a statement that is not absolutely true for every person on the planet, it's a signal that you need to question it. There are plenty of people who don't cook for their husbands and don't feel guilty. It's not a universal truth. The coach continued:

"It sounds as though the way you have this set up in your mind is that you either cook for him and feel resentful and get frustrated, or you take a chance and not cook for him and you may or may not feel guilty. Now the choice is yours. What would you like to do?"

When you reach the point in the conversation when your client recognizes their pain and suffering they are currently experiencing versus the fear of going to the desired change, you have reached the leverage point.

The choice you present to your client at this point is not an easy one because it means they have to give up a long-held idea. Silence is critical — wait for their answer! They're not likely to say, in Christina's case, "Oh sure, I can stop cooking for him." She has to really think, "What will happen if I stop cooking for him? What if I stop and it's okay?"

You *cannot* move forward until your client is ready to choose. They will respond in some way. No matter what they decide, whether to continue as is, to change their thinking, or to take action, you have to accept it. In this case Christina said, "I'm going to take that chance and not cook for him every night." That's an action step that occurred organically.

LOOK FOR A RETURN TO THE FAMILIAR

Fear is a natural reaction to moving closer to the truth.
— Pema Chodron

When a client arrives at the leverage point, they typically run back to their original position — that which is comfortable. The leverage point is filled with fear and limiting ideas, thoughts, and beliefs that subconsciously keep them from naturally moving forward. They think, "Ugh, this is too hard. I can't do this — nah, I don't think so," and they turn back. That's the arrow pointing back to the starting place. In their experience, every time they start moving toward what they want, something gets in the way, and *boom*, they go back to the zone where things are familiar, even though it's miserable. If you've ever started a fitness plan, made some initial progress, and then stopped, you've encountered this tendency to return to a familiar position.

When your client returns to their current position, it can be because they have devised a temporary strategy they think is working, the fear takes over, their motivation isn't strong enough, or there is no compelling vision pulling them forward. Despite the client believing they want something different from what they have, they're not motivated to do what it takes to make the change.

It's up to you to point out that the current situation is actually causing pain and not serving them. Until your client can accept this, they won't be motivated to move past the leverage point toward what they really want. If they stay where things are comfortable, they will not be challenged, experience personal growth, or learn new things. In other words, they will stagnate.

THE SHIFT

There are several techniques for facilitating a shift. Any one of them works well and some may lend themselves more to one situation than another. Following the details of the various methods that follow are some clues that a shift has taken place and then how to proceed from that point.

There is a particular series of questions that has often proven to be highly effective in facilitating a shift even though I advise against formulaic coaching and standardized questions. Each question deepens the client's awareness. It is important to note that if you consistently choose the same method in the same way, it *is* a formula.

This question helps the client realize the pain of inertia:

"What is it costing you to..."

[Finish this question using the exact words your client used.]

161

For example, "What is it costing you *to think you're the only one who can do it?*" You will then typically hear a "laundry list" of things your client already knows: it's costing them sleep, energy, health, time, etc. I encourage you to write down what they share; you will need this data for your next question. Repeat the question above using your client's words. For example:

"You said it costs you mental energy, not enough time with your family, and exhaustion.

What *else* is it costing you to think you're the only one who can do it?"

[Include the entire statement they claim after "What else is it costing you...?"]

Your client will now have to go deeper and think of something they likely haven't already thought about. When you include all the words from their answer, it not only helps them remember their answers, but also has a more profound impact to spur deeper thinking.

Your client will likely have to think before responding. Again, remain silent and give them the space to think. Then they might say something like, "It's limiting my life to the point where I dread each day." Sometimes obliging the client to think at this deeper level allows them to realize in that moment that they must make a change. They're admitting just how bad things really are beyond what they already acknowledged.

Depending on the depth of their response, another question might solidify just how bad their current situation is. It's about the payoff or benefit of staying in this painful place:

"What do you get out of thinking that you are the only one who can do it?" Or "How does it serve you to think that you are the only one who can do it?"

[Include the entire statement they claim.]

More often than not, your client will answer with something like, "Nothing" or "It doesn't." At that point they believe that there couldn't possibly be a valid reason for holding on to an idea that is obviously filled with negative consequences. But in truth, if there had been no valid reason, even a subconscious one, to hang on to the idea, they would have let it go. That is exactly what needs to be conveyed.

"If you really believed you got nothing out of it [or it doesn't serve you], it wouldn't make sense to keep holding on. There has to be something in it for you *to still think you're the only one who can do it.*"

[Include the entire statement they claim.]

Your client will usually come up with something they hadn't thought about previously, such as "It makes me feel important" or "No one else can do it the way I do."

This is now a place for motivating your client to change. If they absolutely can't think of any possible reason to remain with the bad situation, you can prompt them: "One option might be so that you don't have to face letting go of something you have built from scratch. What do you think it might be?" They might answer something like, "I think my husband would be upset if I started delegating it to others." There is usually an underlying subconscious reason why someone holds on to an idea even if it's obviously holding them back.

For each question, it is crucial to include the entire statement they claim. This makes the question far more impactful, and more importantly, reminds the client what they said.

Here's an example of holding on to an idea:

* * *

Kathryn stated that ten years ago she failed at something, and *since that time it has hindered her achievements and ability to stay focused without overwhelming emotion.* This is the belief she thinks is true. Note that in the following dialogue it's irrelevant to know what the failure was about.

163

Coach: What is it costing you to hold on to the memory of that failure?

Kathryn: My health, enjoyment, extending happiness to other people, it slows my pace, achieving goals, and it hinders my abilities and strengths.

Coach: What *else* is it costing you to hold on to the memory of that failure?

Kathryn: [After a pause] I've lost some friendships and I feel overwhelming sadness. I'm the type of person who likes to connect with people and achieving is important to me.

Coach: If it's costing your health, enjoyment, extending happiness to other people, it slows your pace, achieving goals, it hinders your abilities and strengths, lost friendships, and overwhelming sadness, what has you holding on so tightly to this past memory?

Kathryn: I can't help it because my emotions overwhelm everything.

Coach *[recognizing that the last statement is not the truth]*: Emotions will always come up, but we do have control as to what we do with them. What do you want to do?

Kathryn: Now I'm smiling because I realize I don't have to let that memory take over my life because something happened ten years ago. After saying that, I can let go of the past and probably have better connections and more achievements.

When Kathryn realized everything that her belief was costing her, she shifted her thinking and gained a new perspective.

MORE WAYS TO CREATE A SHIFT

- Remove the *perceived* obstacle:
  Client: I have no time for my business because of all of my doctor's appointments.
  Coach: What would be different with your business if you didn't have any doctor's appointments?

- Discrepancy or disconnect:
  Client: At one point the idea seemed exceptional and now it's sounding ordinary.
  Coach: What has changed?

- Far-fetched analogy:
  Client: I feel so awful because my co-worker told me I was a slow worker.
  Coach: What if your friend told you she didn't like the way you dress for work?

  Client: That would be just silly.
  Coach: What's different about that and your co-worker's opinion about your work?

- Challenge questions:
  Client: I'm afraid to speak up when I'm in a group of peers, although I really want to get better at contributing and communicating my ideas.
  Coach: What if speaking up when you're with your peers is one of the best ways to contribute and get better at communicating? What would that mean for you?

Be careful with challenging questions, though. You don't want to convince your client of something that isn't true.

For example, if your client says, "I'm terrible with math and anything to do with numbers. I would rather hire someone to help me with my financial affairs than attempt it on my own," be careful not to ask, "What makes you think you can't do it on your own?"

165

This isn't a proper challenge and may cause frustration because it appears to be factual, not opinion or self-assessment.

- Direct communication:

  Client: My assistant has been absent this year more often than she shows up, and because I'm so afraid of conflict, I don't say anything. I just don't want to lose her.

  Coach: In some ways it sounds as though you have already lost her. What do you think?

REFRAMING

Although reframes don't necessarily go as deep as a true shift in perspective, they help a client move forward by providing a new interpretation of a long-held idea that has held them back.

Reframing is seeing the same set of facts in an entirely different way due to receiving added information. Unfortunately, we often make interpretations with limited amounts of information and then stick to our conclusion despite the additional information. It's a coach's responsibility to reframe a statement when it's inhibiting progress and getting a client to change their fixed interpretation is part of a process.

Here's an example to illustrate reframing:

* * *

Imagine that I'm walking down the street and I meet a woman I haven't seen in over ten years. We start chatting, having a lovely conversation. She tells me that she just purchased shoes for $800 at a high-end department store.

STOP: [Just hearing that piece of information, what are you thinking at this moment? Most people form an opinion or make a judgment.]

The story continues. Now she tells me she just found out that she won millions of dollars in the lottery, and that she has decided to make one totally frivolous purchase.

[What are you thinking about her purchase now? Perhaps something more along the lines of "That's not a very frivolous purchase considering she won so much money" or "I wonder how much money she won?" or "What has her sharing this information?" Your opinion is reframed as the story moves along.]

The conversation continues, and she tells me she's going to donate millions of her winnings to charity and she's currently in the process of researching various charities.

It's more than likely you have a very different opinion of this woman now than at the start of the conversation. The point is, if you draw conclusions before having enough data, the conversation can easily go down the wrong path, especially in coaching.

In this particular story, we took a fact, added some more data, and wound up seeing the facts in a different way. She still bought $800 shoes, but now we view her differently. We have to remove the tendency to draw an early conclusion when coaching and learn to reframe based on potential additional data that changes the complexion of the story.

Reframing can also separate fact from perception. And it can remove some of the stress and emotion from a client's interpretation of a situation. This is best explained using this example:

Little Timmy was standing at the top of a ladder. His father, noticing Timmy had a fear of heights, told him to jump and he would catch him. Without hesitation, Timmy leapt off the ladder, his father stepped back, and Timmy fell to the ground.

What do you think happened in the story?

Here are some possible initial interpretations:

- The father was trying to teach Timmy a lesson.
- The father is mean and cruel.
- Timmy was betrayed.
- The father stepped back on purpose.

Here are the facts of the story:

- Timmy was on a ladder.
- Timmy jumped.
- Timmy's father was there and took a step back.
- Timmy fell to the ground.

Suppose Timmy grows up, and now he's Tim, and he hires you and says, "My father is a liar and he never really cared about me. When I was a little kid, I was up on a ladder and Dad told me that I should jump and he would catch me. Instead, he stepped back and let me fall to the ground, so he is a liar and obviously didn't really care about me." Can you see how Tim might come to you with that story? Can you see how people draw conclusions based on past experience?

Be aware that many clients don't know how to distinguish fact from perception. *Your role is to reframe so your client can see the same set of facts in a different way.* I use a simple but powerful phrase for reframing — *if used correctly*:

"Is it possible that...?"

Just as effective (and not a yes/no) is the phrase "What if you knew that...?"

After using one of these phrases you present a potentially different conclusion based on the same facts. You are not trying to change your client's mind but rather nudge them or jar their thinking a bit so that it's difficult for them to stick to their original conclusion with the same intensity. This might open them to other possibilities.

For example, in the above story, suppose Tim says, "My father is a liar and he let me fall to the ground, and he never liked me, and now look what he's doing to me. It hasn't changed after all these years."

You ask, "Well, Tim, *is it possible that* at the moment you jumped, your father's depth perception was off, and he took a step back thinking that was where he would catch you, and he was wrong?" Or,

"What if you knew that his intention was to catch you, but his depth perception was off?" You can make up any interpretation, like:

- At the moment you jumped, he sneezed.
- At the moment you jumped, somebody pulled him away from behind.
- At the moment you jumped, he was startled by a loud noise.

It doesn't matter what you make up, 99 percent of the time the client will say, *"Nope, that wasn't what happened, that isn't possible."*

Then you repeat your interpretation, because in actuality, it's the client's belief, not a fact. "So, Tim, I know that you don't think so, but *is it possible* that your father's depth perception was off, and he thought he was going to catch you?"

Tim replies, *"Well, I guess that's possible. I don't think that's what happened, but I guess it's possible."* Just that slim acceptance on Tim's part is enough to reduce the intensity of his 100-percent "this is it" thinking.

Reframing using questions can also help your client see something obvious that they're missing, but in reality is right in front of them. Take this life-changing reframe:

* * *

Mark told me how much he loved to play basketball but that it was too frustrating because he's just 5'5". He wanted to participate in the game, but because of his height he rarely, if ever, got the ball. He always felt dominated by the taller players.

The question I asked that reframed his thinking was "What would it be like to assemble a team of shorter men who also enjoy playing basketball so that there is no height problem?" Mark had honestly never thought of that option, and truly believed his only choice was to give up basketball and play a different sport instead.

169

Asking a question that offers a different perspective without making a suggestion can reshape someone's thinking.

I remember telling a friend about something another friend had done that was disturbing me, and she asked, "Marion, is it possible that he was just too tired?" I replied, "Oh no, not possible." And she asked, "But Marion, *is it possible* that he was too tired?" And I had to concede because I don't know what really happened. I was making it up. It was my story, my invention. So when she asked, "Is it possible" a second time, I had to say, "It is possible." And as soon as I admitted that, I could feel the tension leave me, even though I still didn't know what really happened. Opening my mind just that tiny, tiny crack to another interpretation took away the intensity of "This is how it is."

WHEN NOT TO REFRAME

There's a big caveat that goes with this technique: Your client might not be looking for a new interpretation. It can get obnoxious to keep reframing when that's the case. Use it only when your client is stuck on something and it is preventing them from moving forward. If it's not invited, it's not welcome. You don't reframe for everyone with whom you talk. You reframe when somebody's really stuck in an interpretation and it's getting in their way of moving forward.

WHEN THE CLIENT IS NOT WILLING TO LET GO OF THEIR BELIEF

On rare occasions, clients are just not ready or able to give up on something they believe. This is particularly true when it's based on a value such as, "Always be good to other people." Even a great-sounding value like that can be detrimental to a client's well-being if the sacrifices they're making are taking a toll on their health. You don't want to force your client to let go of a limiting idea, but you can help them realize that their thinking is not serving or benefiting them in the best way possible by pointing out their complaints or dissatisfaction with how things are. Once they become aware of this, they should become at least *motivated* to consider doing something different.

CLUES THAT A SHIFT HAS TAKEN PLACE

A shift can take place at any point in a coaching conversation. It's not necessarily one big "Aha!" Through reflection and direct communication, often shifts take place throughout the coaching conversation. Here are some clues that a shift has taken place:

- Your client says, "Hmmmm...," perhaps followed by a lot of out-loud processing.
- Your client's voice changes — louder, softer, they laugh, they're more energetic, etc.
- There is silence or a long pause after a question, indicating deep thinking.
- Your client says something like, "I never thought of it that way before."

LOOPING

At the point in the conversation at which it appears that a change in thinking or feeling (shift) has taken place, looping is appropriate. *Looping* means connecting your client's initial emotion or desire to the current place in the conversation. It provides an opportunity for clients to reflect on their progress, summarize their awareness, and realize how much has changed since the conversation began.

The "loop" is a barometer for ascertaining where things are, how much more your client needs, and if they've reached a point of saturation. It demonstrates collaboration and partnering between you and your client.

Here's a simple looping question: "At the beginning of our conversation you were [confused/frustrated/annoyed/wondering/hoping for a decision]. Where are you at this point?" This is a masterful way to ask your client to do the summary and to let you know how much has been absorbed and integrated. This also provides a clue as to how much may be needed for the remainder of the conversation. Most often following a distinct shift, it is time to begin closing down the conversation.

You can loop at any point in the conversation, especially when you're feeling lost and you're not sure how to proceed: "Up until now we've been talking about X. What would be helpful at this point?"

Contrary to what I often hear, it is *not* up to the coach to summarize and tell the client what's been discussed. Having your client tell you how much has been absorbed and what has changed for them is more informative as opposed to what you believe your client has taken away from the conversation.

The majority of what clients share in their summary is about what has changed regarding the *situation*. Therefore, it's beneficial to ask a follow-up question such as "What have you learned about yourself?" This question is often welcomed by your client and spurs them to think on a deeper level.

Your client might answer something like this: "Now that I realize that having the conversation is easier than I anticipated, I'm going to work tomorrow looking forward to it instead of dreading it." When an action step and a time frame are organically revealed, your coaching likely has gone deep enough, and it may not be necessary to delve deeply into accountability. Typically, between looping and/or the follow-up question, you will hear built-in action(s).

MISSING THE SHIFT

As you will discover, going beyond the shift with more probing questions can be detrimental, and it's one of the biggest mistakes in coaching.

The shift can manifest when your client gets quiet and then says, "OMG, I feel so much better now, I really get it. I need to…"

This is when you honor that your client is stopping to reflect — the saturation point. Your client is likely processing and is possibly in an emotional state of mind and can't take in anything else from that point on. Continuing to question can only serve *you* at this point and takes your client out of feeling present and puts them back into their head. You will check in with your client throughout the conversation, but as I explained earlier, it's important to ask a looping question after a change in voice, tone, pace, an *aha!* moment, or a laugh.

Of course, sometimes there is no shift or *aha!* moment during the conversation. The shift often occurs between sessions when the client has time to thoroughly process the conversation.

Alternatively, sometimes the shift can come early in the conversation and the coach keeps going because they feel an obligation to give the full allotted time to their client. It doesn't necessarily take a lot to shift somebody, and the conversation can be rather short. The client will still receive tremendous value and will likely feel complete despite the short time frame, and it's vital to check in to see where they are and what they want to do. They are often content to stop the coaching and get into action. *Coaching is not about time; it's about providing value.*

A shift in thinking can be one of the most powerful experiences your client will feel. Sometimes just getting new information can totally shift their thinking.

MUFFING THE SHIFT

It is very easy for the coaching conversation to go awry during this part of the conversation. I've heard the following mistakes from coaches when facilitating a shift:

- Believing that what the client says is the truth for them
- Not believing that the ideas around the change are created by limited thinking
- Knowing when to point out the pain in the current situation

- Creating an alternative way of looking at a limiting belief rather than creating a new perspective
- Not figuring out the underlying main belief (idea) that is keeping the client stuck
- Not exploring the person deeply enough — too much emphasis on the situation
- Thinking that the client's fear is justified
- Not recognizing that the ultimate desire is not anchored in the client's truth
- Judging the client's limiting beliefs as foolish or unfounded

If you keep in mind "Don't believe the client," you're already honing your skill of curiosity. Your focus should be on listening for what is true and what is perception so you can help them figure out what is true *for this person* so they can move forward.

Be aware that providing a plausible reframe or facilitating a shift may take practice. It's a new kind of conversation for most people. A good starting place is to listen for the leverage point and identify the "faulty thinking." You will improve your abilities over time, and you may struggle as you learn. Don't be too hard on yourself — it becomes easier with experience.

QUESTIONS FOR REFLECTION

- What are some of the ways to create a shift that you are willing to try?
- What are your thoughts about the idea that 90 percent of people move away from pain while only 10 percent move toward pleasure? What affect might that have on your coaching?
- What do you think about your client's action step being organically born out of a true shift in thinking, thereby making detailed accountability unnecessary?

PART IV: THE END

CHAPTER 11

MOVING FORWARD AND CLOSING THE CONVERSATION

If everyone is moving forward together, then success takes care of itself.
— Henry Ford

THE ANATOMY OF A COACHING CONVERSATION			
	THE BEGINNING	THE MIDDLE	THE END
Laser-Focused Mindset	1) Opening question 2) Client story 3) First question *after story* 4) Agreement	5) Discerning truth from perception 6) The shift / change in perspective 7) Looping	8) Optional bonus question 9) Support (resources) 10) Closing and championing

The final element of any conversation is the closing. Partnership must be demonstrated throughout the coaching session and is particularly important in the latter portion. The client is in "processing" mode after all of the coaching and is ready to implement what they are taking away. If the coaching got to the deeper place, the client has automatically created their own step(s) for forward movement.

BONUS QUESTION

After the client has experienced a shift, you'll reach the saturation point where it's best to move towards completing the session. You'll usually be able to tell when your client's thinking has changed because they will sound more upbeat, relaxed, or relieved. However, if you still hear or sense any hesitancy regarding moving forward, it is appropriate to ask about a potential obstacle that might prevent them from taking action: "What might stop you from...?"

If, however, the client seems ready to move forward and you've already "looped" and asked them what they learned about themselves, you may consider wrapping up with a bonus question to explore how their new perspective might impact other areas of their life. This question can broaden the scope of the conversation and client discovery. For example, "Now that you realize that setting boundaries was a problem, where else in your life do you see that happening?"

As long as your question doesn't put a damper on your client's emotional state, it's justified. Remember that after there's been a shift, many clients are "cooked, fried, and done" and are not open for more thinking questions or detailed follow-up. Therefore, assess the client's emotional state to determine if the bonus question would add value.

ENDING THE SESSION — ESTABLISH SUPPORT

Once you realize that your client has gained something and feels relatively complete, and their plan has been organically stated, it's important to help them use their environment to support them.

A question such as "Is there somebody or something that can support you [now that you know what you want to do / as you prepare for what you're going to do]?" is important because, moving forward, you want them to rely on someone in their life besides you. The intention is for your client to create their own supportive environment and their own resources to further their agreed-upon action(s).

Your client might say something like "I'll talk to my husband tonight about this" or "I can check in with my sister when I get home," addressing *who* will help them; or "I just need to journal" or "I just need to sit with it," addressing *what* will help them. If they say they don't need any outside help, that may be perfectly reasonable.

FOSTER FORWARD MOVEMENT

If your client's shift is deep enough to change their thinking, almost every time they will automatically create their own plan or action. They will be naturally motivated to want to make changes to incorporate their new perspective. This, of course, is the ideal.

However, if forward movement doesn't arise naturally, you should offer support as they move forward into new behaviors. Collaborate with them in exploring options to create forward movement. Their actions should be congruent with the level of the client and the nature of their situation. Your role is to empower and build confidence, intuition, and sustainable growth.

PARTNER AND COLLABORATE

It is appropriate to partner with your client (or allow your client solely) to design actions or thinking that align with their desired outcomes that will take place after the session. Your approach should not be *parental* as opposed to *collaborative*.

Parental means assigning them something to do as though you're their parent making sure they do their homework. For example, you ask, "Are you willing to try something this week?" When they say yes, you say, "Great. Here's what I'd like you to do." That's the parent talking to the child.

In *collaboration*, you and your client determine how they want to be accountable. Some coaches fall into the trap of feeling responsible for creating action plans and/or micromanaging their client's progress. Not only does this imply that their client isn't a capable adult, but it also implies that the coach doesn't trust their client's stated commitment. Hopefully, you won't be tempted to be the sole support person to manage your client's progress, but rather recognize that helping your client create their own supportive environment is far more practical and useful as they go forward.

INVITE YOUR CLIENT TO EXPERIMENT

Coaches often ask clients to do work outside of the coaching session. They call this *homework, field work, assignment, action step(s), inquiries,* etc. My preference is to avoid any term that conjures up thoughts of school. The word *experiment* can be more invitational and suggests that something may or may not work. It removes the pressure to perform.

Actions don't have to be *doing* something. They can be thinking or creating, and sometimes they can be *not* doing anything. Sometimes just leaving your client where they are is fine, depending on the situation. Clients may not respond well to being asked to do something such as journal or draw. It's always prudent to ask your client what *they* think would be most helpful.

* * *

Bill is a client who is always doing, doing, doing. He always has to have something on his to-do list; always has to be busy. Although he asks for an action step, it might be helpful to ask, "What do you think about the idea of doing *nothing* for one day?" Sometimes doing nothing is a great experiment.

SET UP YOUR CLIENT FOR SUCCESS

Because each client is unique, some are enthusiastic and willing to make major changes quickly, while others are overwhelmed by demands and require a slower pace. The following examples demonstrate some approaches tailored to individual clients:

Jasmine wants to change her career and become an interior designer. Having no experience, she wonders what a typical week would look like.

Coach: What might be a good way to find out?

Jasmine: Asking someone in the field or doing research would help.

Coach: How many people would it make sense for you to contact this week to talk to about getting some of your questions answered?

Jasmine: I think I could talk with one person.

Coach (*using the client as a barometer*): Would you be willing, as an experiment, just for the coming week, to talk with two people?

If the coach had asked, "What about talking with ten people?" chances are Jasmine wouldn't have made any calls, based on her offer to make just one call. It's one thing to stretch a client; it's another to ask for too much (or too little). Use your client's response to gauge how much or how little to challenge.

* * *

Angela wants to increase the number of times she exercises in a week.

Coach: How many times do you think it makes sense for you to exercise?

Angela: I'm going to try it every day in the coming week.

Coach: That sounds like a huge commitment. What about at least three times in the coming week?

The coach wants Angela to succeed and not feel burdened. Angela will probably exercise more than three times but not as many as seven. It's important to stretch the client, but you can also give them permission to do less so they can succeed.

> *To empower your client, let them suggest a step — and frequency, if relevant — and then using your client's suggestion as a gauge, consider adjusting their action plan up or down to ensure success.*

Most often, clients automatically report their progress without any prompts. That said, if you believe that the agreed-upon action didn't occur, it's your role to inquire as to what got in the way.

In my early days of coaching, before I learned to consistently get to the deeper shifts that naturally generate an action, I asked clients to consider doing their suggested action just for the coming week. This cut down on their feeling overwhelmed and made it easier for them to make it an ingrained habit that continued far beyond the initial week.

CLOSE THE COACHING SESSION

Closing the coaching session must be a collaborative effort, and it must give your client the opportunity to say whether or not they're finished and if there's anything else they need. It shouldn't be a decision the coach makes unilaterally.

A question that demonstrates collaboration would be, "Is there anything else that might be helpful on this topic [or in this conversation]?" or, "Is this a good place for us to stop?" It is critical to include the words "on this topic" or "in this conversation" so your client doesn't start a brand-new topic. This closing allows them to have equal say in whether or not it's time to end.

If your client says, "Oh! There's just one more thing!" at this point, in fairness to them it's okay to ask what the topic is and then make a decision. (You might have heard this called the "doorknob syndrome"; time is up, and your client just remembered another topic.) You might be able to quickly discuss it. Either it's appropriate to address because it will only take a moment, or it's more appropriate to say something like "That sounds like a whole other conversation. We're going to have to hold that."

CHAMPION INSTEAD OF CHEERLEAD

Remind people who they are instead of just complimenting them on what they've done.
— Thomas J. Leonard

If you can be *genuinely* supportive during the conversation, clients feel validated. It is not appropriate to cheerlead by saying something like "Wow!" or "Awesome work!"

Finally, somewhere at the end of the conversation, when your client has processed a great deal, you have another opportunity to champion your client for the progress made.

Your comment should include context so it is affirming: "You certainly have done a great deal of work to realize how important X is to you." Or, "I want to acknowledge that this problem was very convoluted and intricate, and yet you stayed with it."

PUTTING IT ALL TOGETHER

Below is a Laser-Focused Coaching phone conversation incorporating everything I've discussed so far. This includes distilling the story, getting to the root of the problem, and creating a permanent solution. You will notice the elements from the anatomy of a coaching conversation throughout. I include my thoughts and reasoning to highlight key principles of Laser-Focused Coaching.

Marion (the coach): Wilma, we have about thirty minutes. What is it that we can focus on today that will make a difference for you?

Wilma (the client): Okay, so, where do I start? Remember last week I shared that we had a mini-flood in the house and that got fixed. And then on Sunday we had a mini-fire in the house. Everybody's fine, and just a closet got charred. That just gives you the context of why now everything has become "I can't deal, like don't give me one more thing."

So, the story is, I have this one woman that I've known a long, long time, back when I used to teach, and she was one of my best students. She was wonderful at everything, and had many good qualities, except the check never came, you know? And it was one of those things.

And I lived in the same city probably fifty blocks away from her. And she would say to me that the post office where she lived was really, really slow, and that was the reason that check never came.

183

So, you know, excuses, excuses, excuses. So, it was very annoying. I eventually switched gears and we lost track.

We rekindled our connection a little bit later. She produced [popular TV show] for a long time, and she decided, after she left TV, to start her own business and help people do public speaking. So somehow, we got reconnected and she told me that she was doing that, and I said, "Well, you know, I do have some coaching clients who could use a service like that." And she said, "Oh, great, maybe we can do a referral service, and I refer people to you for coaching, and you'll refer people to me for public speaking, and I'll give you a commission and you'll give me a commission." So, we started, and actually I gave her quite a few clients and she was supposed to send me the commission check. But it was like pulling teeth.

It was always something. It took months and months to get paid, which really annoyed the hell out of me. And I was like thinking, you know, "Why am I doing this anyway?" Anyway, I was getting very annoyed.

So recently I gave her another client for only one session, and it was maybe three months ago. I still haven't gotten the check. And of course, I asked for it, and she wrote back and said, "Check is on the way." That was four weeks ago. And I said, "The check? I haven't seen it." Then she just sent me this email yesterday saying, "Oh, I'm so sorry, your check was in a pile that I was going to mail, but my mother, who lives in another state and is ninety, broke her hip, and I had to go there and now I'm back. I don't have your address to send the check." I am so annoyed at this point. I couldn't help but say, "How did you send me a check before? My address hasn't changed, but here it is again."

I wanted to ask her a different question, something not related to coaching at all. We're supposed to speak after this call, and you know, part of me is wondering, "Do I really need this?" It's like I don't know if this is working for me, and it's really pushing my buttons. Of course, it doesn't help that I'm in a little bit of a vulnerable position with all this water and fire damage in the house. But I'm just questioning, a little bit: what am I doing here? So that's my story.

Marion: Wilma, I'm really sorry about all of the immediate awful things that have happened in your house. And it seems that this unresponsive woman is really draining you. And yet, you had a lot of warning early on and still continued. I'm just wondering, what is that about?

[I acknowledged her house problems and then went right to the heart of the matter by sharing an observation and questioning Wilma's behavior. Quickly identifying boundaries (accepting unacceptable behavior) as the theme helped to create the first question.]

Wilma: I seem to be a very slow learner. It's a lot of repetition before I really learn my lesson and just really get the fact that this may not be the situation or relationship that's working.

Marion: All right. So then, what is it that would be really helpful for you in our conversation?

[In this rare instance, I had no clue what she wanted, thus this question early on.]

Wilma: Hmm. To know how to not to get into so much repeat. To just get this early warning sign, like you said, and then to just cut the ties sooner rather than later. And also, I'm going to have a conversation with her, not knowing what to say. And you know, as much as I don't want it to be competitive, I don't have to tell her all my referrals for the coaching year, but maybe I should, I don't know. I mean how to handle my annoyance maybe.

Marion: I'm hearing how annoyed you say you are with this woman, and it sounds more like there's real annoyance with yourself. What's true about that?

Wilma: Yes, it seems that I am angry with myself. It seems to be a pattern, and I don't want to repeat it over and over. It's enough already. I want to know how to cut ties and to notice the early warning signs.

Marion: Wilma, I can understand that you want to avoid this mess going forward. What do you think would be helpful in figuring out how to notice early warning signs? *[Deepening the agreement]*

Wilma: Wow, that's a very tough question. Well, I have to say, you were very, very insightful in saying yes, the annoyance is with myself as much as it is with her, maybe more with myself. And so, what would I… what would be helpful in… what was the end of the question, what would be helpful in getting early signs?

Marion: What do you think might help you figure out how to notice these early warning signs? *[Further deepening the agreement]*

Wilma: I think I have to have less tolerance for them, for this. Not just for the sign, for the behavior, like right away, as opposed to how I always give people another chance and another chance and then it explodes. That's my usual MO. After X amount of times while I allow you to step on my foot, I just then go, "Wait a second." And then you don't know whatever happened to you, because I'm just like way overboard. Because it was so bottled up. So maybe it's about expressing it early on.

Marion: Mm-hmm.

Wilma: I think I have in some ways, but you know, some people just don't listen. They just, you know, they ignore. And this woman is one of them.
["Some people just don't listen" was a clue that she was blaming and not taking any responsibility.]

Marion: You know what this reminds me of? When people say to their dog, "Fido, get over here. Fido, come on Fido, we have to go home. Come here." You've heard that, right? And then you hear somebody else in a stern voice say, "Fido, now! We're going home!" When you hear this example, what do you think about your delivery? *[The example demonstrated a distinction she could hear.]*

Wilma: I'm sure there is something about that, because, you know, I feel if I have to send you three emails to get my check that you should get that I'm annoyed. So, but you know, they're not reading my mind, they don't care. And this woman is a bully, and she'll just go out of her way to just drag her feet about things. So yes, she's not hearing; she's not hearing because I'm not saying, "Where's my freaking check?" I don't know. How would I say it? That's what I need help with. It's like I felt I said it, but obviously I have not said it properly. How would I say it?

[Despite this question, note the following deflection and another distinction regarding the delivery of her message.]

Marion: Mm-hmm. There's what I call the namby-pamby, wishy-washy, "Oh, I'm not happy. I don't like what's going on here." Or, "I'm not going to tolerate this!" There's a big difference. So, based on what you said — "But I tell them, and they just don't listen" — what would it mean for you if you were so clear that "I need that check, or we are finished"?

Wilma: Scary. Because even though I'm, you know, a tough cookie and everything, and I'm a single mum with three kids so I have to be, part of me feels like you have to be kind and you have to be nice. And part of my culture is not about cut and dry like that. So it just feels a little bit scary to cut ties this severely. But yeah, you know?

Marion: So now we have the balance between "I can keep doing it the way I've been doing it — being the nice guy; getting annoyed all the time, stepped on, and bullied; and keep giving and giving while she's taking" or "I can take a chance, as scary as it might be saying something like, 'Hey listen, I've had enough, I need to cut ties' and maybe it will be effective, and she will be okay with it, and maybe she won't." What do you want to do?

[It is important to acknowledge the leverage point. Notice how much relevant data follows.]

Wilma: No, I mean I don't want to respond with another long thing, but I just have to add, yes, of course. I don't want to be the... I want to stop being the nice person, because that doesn't work for me. And in a setting that I just had an ex-boyfriend in the same week that I had the water and the fire and everything, I had to ask for an order of protection, and they put a restraining order on him because he could not hear. And I had been saying for a year and a half the same things. And he kept on coming and he kept on trying to see me, and he kept on sending email. I had to go to the police to basically have them intervene, and they felt like it was escalating, and they needed to intervene. But see, but maybe the extent of how helpless I am when in a situation like that. So yeah, I need to fix it. *[Notice how the theme of boundaries also shows up elsewhere in her life.]*

Marion: Okay. In the case of this woman, what do you want to do?

Wilma: I would like to have the right language to tell her that this is not acceptable.

Marion: If you could say anything you wanted to say to her with no consequences, what would you want to say?

Wilma: I would say that, "You know, unless things are done in a timely manner…," but that doesn't seem strong enough.

Marion: No, it doesn't. It still sounds like the nice guy. Don't be the nice person. Just what would you *really* want to say? *[Since Wilma didn't answer it the first time, it was repeated, and it still didn't get answered.]*

Wilma: "Give me the check right away. Once you're getting paid, just don't make me ask you by three emails to get my money. Otherwise I don't want to work with you."

Marion: Sounds strong and with conviction. Now, how can you say that so she can hear it?

Wilma: So, I would say, you know, "I've really appreciated working with you. The clients we've had, and we've shared, they benefited from your public speaking, coaching, and I need this relationship to get in better shape in terms of your paying my commission. And…"

Marion: I wish you could see my face. My face is saying, "You've got to be kidding."

Wilma: I need help with the language.

Marion: All right. What do you *really* want to say? *[Again, repeating the question.]*

Wilma: "I need to be paid a week after the coaching happens," and then she says she will, but I don't feel that way, but I don't care. "I just need to be paid the week after or there will be no more referrals."

Marion: So now, what are you going to say to her?

Wilma: Can I just say what I just said?

Marion: Yes.

Wilma: Okay. That's I want to say to her.

Marion: Considering that we started the conversation with your frustration, where are things now with figuring out the early warning signs?
[After her tone changed, it was an opportunity to loop and see where things stood.]

Wilma: I have no idea, I don't know. That's a tough one, you know, because there's that, if somebody is doing it once, does that constitute enough of a warning sign, or do I have to wait for the second?

Marion: What do you think?

Wilma: I think once is enough.

Marion: It's up to you.

Wilma: You know, the only thing is, as we're talking and you're telling me, I just get butterflies in my stomach. It's just so difficult for me to do that. You know, it's so dumb. I mean, I probably sound like a major idiot. But it's just, you know, I always want to give people some slack.

Marion: Fair enough. Then the question becomes, just how much slack? *[Notice how I didn't get hooked by her "major idiot" statement and go off on a tangent.]*

Wilma: Less slack than I have in the past. Yes. There is a cost involved of course. And for my clients I would say, "What's the cost?" Of course, but I just, you know, it's very, for some reason it's hard for me to do. I don't know. And this is a recurring theme in my life, I feel like I've never set a consequence.

Marion: What are you afraid of if you are really clear with somebody and have a consequence?
[A chance to find out what the fear had been all along and deepen her awareness.]

Wilma: That they go away.

Marion: And?

Wilma: Yeah really, and big deal. They need to go away if they don't listen. I know, I know. It's the people-pleasing. I don't know what it is, aside from the people-pleasing.

Marion: Uh-huh. So the fear is they go away. And as you've said, these are people who should go away. Is there somebody or something that could help you as you learn to set these boundaries or recognize these warning signs?
[Outside resources to create her own supportive environment]

Wilma: Unfortunately, I think this is a thing that I just have to do on my own and be accountable for. I don't see anybody that can help me with this, because it's between me and whomever. All the theory in the world obviously has not really moved the needle much. Because I know the theory. So, it's just implementing that I have to practice.

Marion: Wilma, what have you learned about yourself in all of this?

Wilma: I have been too afraid, you know, of setting a consequence. I've let people... I have given too much slack. When I notice that someone isn't listening to me, I have to tell them that I really mean it. Up to now, I thought I was doing that. Now I know that I really wasn't. It will still feel a little scary, but I know I have to do it.

Marion: When people set clear boundaries, in the beginning, because it's so new, it probably will feel a bit scary. However, after doing it for a while, it gets much easier. What do you think about that?
[Important to "normalize" anticipated fear and question her thoughts.]

Wilma: That's good to know. I want to practice because I'm tired of the same thing over and over again. I know I have to do it differently. I'm glad I can start right after this call and see how it goes.

Marion: That sounds like real progress in changing your pattern. Is there anything else that you need right now for this conversation?
[Collaborative ending]

Wilma: You want to call this woman for me?

Marion: I have no problem doing that. But you need the practice.
[Laughter]

Wilma: Thank you, this was great, and very, very helpful. And really interesting insights and observations and everything was said very well.

Marion: And thank you, Wilma, for your willingness to face this head on. It's been going on for quite some time, and now it seems that with some practice, you can avoid some of these ugly situations.
[Champion client's progress.]

Wilma: Yes, I'm excited to finally do it differently. *[End]*

As you can see, my outline for the beginning, middle, and end of a coaching session keeps your coaching focused on what's really important and is easily customizable for individual clients. You'll create your own questions and reflections for each part of the coaching conversation, and if you follow this overall outline, you'll laser in efficiently and effectively on what's most important for each of your clients. More importantly, you'll focus on the person, not their situation. All of the questions were about Wilma, not the situation and not about the other person.

QUESTIONS FOR REFLECTION

- What struggles, if any, do you currently have in closing your coaching sessions?
- What might change if you use your client as a barometer for a measure (the time, frequency, and amount) of action to take going forward?
- What distinctions can you make between championing and cheerleading? What might be different in your coaching knowing this distinction?

PART V:
MASTERFUL COACHING

CHAPTER 12

THE HEART OF DIRECT COMMUNICATION

Tact is the ability to tell someone to go to hell in a way that they look forward to the trip.
— Winston Churchill

There are times in the coaching conversation when it's beneficial to send a very direct message. While it's often modeled and demonstrated, direct communication, specifically how to choose the right words, is not necessarily taught as a separate coaching skill. Yet knowing *how* to say something can be more important than *what* is said.

> When your heart and mind are clear, you are able to speak simply and directly. If you are cluttered with "shoulds," "what ifs," fear, emotion, or judgments, your message is cloudy.

Please note an important distinction: *directive* versus *direct*. *When you are directive, you are* telling or advising, whereas *direct communication* means sharing what you notice or observe from a neutral place and asking for a response.

THE PURPOSE OF DIRECT COMMUNICATION

The purpose of direct communication is to immediately allow your client to see their situation as it actually is. It is an opportunity to share your thoughts, intuition, observations, and feedback *without* judgment, attachment, or criticism. The key is not to be attached: to the outcome of what you think is going on, to being right, or to expecting client agreement with your observation. You should be willing to let go of any possible outcomes. Whether you're right, wrong, or totally off base can help to create awareness in some direction.

Your role is to be a sounding board, to be impartial, and to act as an outside, objective observer. You should remain neutral without becoming emotionally invested or having a subtle agenda. When you use direct communication, you create awareness for your client.

These are some of the fears you might have in using direct communication:

- You will hurt your client's feelings.
- You will offend your client.
- You will get a bad reputation.
- You could be wrong.
- Your client doesn't really want to hear the truth.
- Your client isn't ready to hear the truth.
- It's safer to stay neutral than to express your opinion.
- If you tell your client what to do, you will feel responsible.
- The biggest risk: You will lose your client.

While we're coaching, we have lots of ideas, thoughts, and even judgments going on in our minds. Thoughts can arise like, "That's crazy," "I can't believe he did that," "What was he thinking?" or "That's not what I would do." Our biggest clue for when to use direct communication is when this mind chatter is going on. If we don't share what comes up the minute it arises, every question we ask after that will be tainted with our thoughts and ideas, and it will feel awkward or more difficult to say if we postpone it.

What you do with your mind chatter can make all the difference in effective coaching. "Telling it like it is" is a wonderful concept, but in truth, unless you say what you mean in a way that can be heard by the client, you can cause damage in the relationship.

So the question is: What are we supposed to do with our thoughts and judgments while coaching?

Let's say you have an opinion that divorce is a really terrible thing, or your client is wealthy, and they spend their money in frivolous ways that go completely against your values. If you realize you cannot be objective because your values clash too much with those of your client, you must share that with your client and let them know you're not the best coach for them. But if, for example, you disapprove of divorce and they have come to you about career transition, you may still be able to be objective and work with that client.

In almost every conversation, you're listening for a discrepancy or something that's not necessarily the truth for your client, and that can show up in a variety of ways. It typically comes across as, "I want it but…." Your client says one thing and then later contradicts it, or something they say just doesn't make sense. These are times to use direct communication.

* * *

Lynda was talking about a problem with her boss and how unhappy she was. She provided many details about their relationship and that she was seriously debating leaving the company because of him. Later in the conversation she said, "I can handle things and my boss really is a good guy. I'm feeling good about this, and I'm ready to stop here." Her coach accepted that statement and believed the conversation was now ready to close.

Unfortunately, the coach missed an opportunity to question a discrepancy. He could have asked a question to help Lynda explore why she said something completely different from what she said when the conversation started, opening a rich area to explore. If Lynda really did want to end there, that has to be honored knowing that the topic will likely reoccur at a later time.

197

Let's compare indirect and direct communication during a coaching session:

Fran said, "It seems wrong that I'm taking money for coaching. I don't have that much experience and just recently finished training. Since I don't really know what I'm doing, I feel like a fraud."

Newer coaches tend to use indirect words when replying to this kind of statement. Indirectness can look like:

- Diluting the message
  - "What can you do to feel better?"
  - "How does that make you feel?"
  - "You aren't being authentic. What can you say about that?"
- Beating around the bush: "If you're not feeling good about what you offer, what can you do to change that?"
- Dressing up the wording or being far too wordy: "Just because you don't have a lot of experience and don't feel confident seems to mean that you aren't feeling like you deserve to get paid, and as if another coach would do it better…."
- Ignoring it
  - "What would you like to feel instead?"
  - "What do you want to get from coaching today?"

Your coaching will be much more powerful if you're direct and only change the delivery — not the impact. Saying something like, "It sounds as though there is a feeling of not being authentic, perhaps somewhat like an imposter. What do you think of that?"

When we want to use a "harsh" word such as *victim, imposter,* or *selfish,* it's helpful to first define the word before saying it. It's easier on your client when you say something like, "It sounds as though there is a feeling of powerlessness, the way a victim might feel."

> *Most important: Don't soften or change the message. Instead, soften the delivery.*

* * *

Charlie wanted to remarry. He said, "I've been ready for a year, and I would love to date seriously, but for some reason I'm not making a lot of progress.

My initial interpretation of Charlie's comment was that he wanted something, but it wasn't happening. I had a choice to ask, "What's in the way?" or "If you found a really terrific woman who meets most of your criteria and is ready to take the plunge, what would that mean?" Choosing the second question and adding context seemed more effective because it allowed Charlie to share what was truly in the way.

Charlie replied that if he found the right woman it would mean he would have to give up his freedom and the fun he'd been having hanging out with the guys. It was then that I recognized the theme: 'either/or.'

My *direct communication* to Charlie was, "It sounds as though this is an 'either/or' situation. Either you're single and free or you're tethered and restricted. What else might be possible?"

Charlie's response was, "OMG! If I met the right woman for me, I would still feel free and able go out with the guys. And my guess is that I wouldn't feel such a strong need to go out so much."

Soon after, Charlie began dating seriously and eventually got married.

Another instance when direct communication can be useful is when your client is blaming others.

* * *

Linsey complained that every time she told her direct reports how they messed up and how disappointed she was, they seemed irritated with her. I felt as though she sometimes came across as arrogant, so I said, "I can understand how frustrating it must be for you, and yet, as your coach I sometimes get the sense that a question I ask you feels annoying. What comes up hearing that?"

Direct communication is often misunderstood. Coaches can feel like they're *telling* their client something they don't want to hear, or that they're being so upfront that it will damage the relationship. Instead, they skirt around what really needs to be said for fear of insulting their client.

As part of your role as a coach — the outside, objective observer — you are entitled to share what comes up for you when you hear something that triggers your thinking. When you know, sense, or feel something, you should share it. Coaches tend to say the "nice-nice" thing, and that doesn't get the message across with any impact. While you may not agree with your client's ideas and thoughts, you can be okay with that and still remain neutral and curious.

> ***Never change the impact. Change the delivery.***

Here are three additional examples:

* * *

Jill: I'm planning to take a trip across the country with my children, and I really want them to enjoy their time. Unfortunately, many of my friends and relatives are insisting that we stay with them as we travel. I think we're going to have to visit everyone.

Coach (direct communication): It sounds as though pleasing others is more important than doing what's best for you and your family. What's true about that?

* * *

Peter: I know I shouldn't worry about what other people think, especially when I'm in a group. However, my workplace is so cutthroat, and I worry about looking stupid, so I've decided it feels safer to stay quiet and not say anything, especially when the CEO comes to a staff meeting.

Coach (direct communication — challenge question): What if people thought your being quiet meant you didn't know anything?

$$* * *$$

Kathy: I don't think I'm capable of having that discussion. I don't like conflict, so it's not worth the effort. I'm just going to continue on and feel crappy.

Coach (indirect communication): What makes you think it's going to be conflicting?

Coach (direct communication): What do you think makes conflict worse than feeling crappy all the time?

WHAT WOULD *YOU* SAY TO YOUR CLIENT IF YOU KNEW THERE WERE NO CONSEQUENCES?

Think about how freeing it would be to just share whatever you want to say and there would be no consequences. While in some ways this *is* possible, there are three guidelines to follow:

1. When being direct by offering an observation, feedback, or your intuitive sense, you *must* follow your statement with a question such as:

   - What do you think?
   - What's true about that?
   - What comes to mind when you hear that?
   - What can you say about that?
   - What is it like for you to hear that?

   If you use direct communication, it is *imperative* that you check out your statement with your client. Otherwise, it seems as though you're telling or knowing. It's crucial to give them an opportunity to respond so you can get accurate data.

2. The word *you* should not be part of your statement. It can come across as an accusation or as if you know your client better than they know themselves. This can make them feel defensive.

   Here's an example that is not okay: "You sound angry."

   Instead, say, "It sounds as though there is some anger. What do you think?"

   Or

   "I'm getting a sense that there might be a feeling of anger. What comes up when you hear that?

   Notice that taking the word *you* out, prevents it from sounding like an accusation.

3. *Own* your observation, feedback, or intuition while being loving and respectful. You're not telling your client about their behavior, thought, or emotion or criticizing it, but rather sharing how it comes across to you. Offer your observation as a supposition so they can agree, disagree, or add new data. For example:

   • From my viewpoint…
   • It seems as though…
   • The way I see it… (The way I hear it…)
   • It sounds as though…
   • I'm getting a sense that…
   • I'm noticing something…

In the above examples, it's clearly your opinion rather than a statement of fact or telling your client what's going on.

> *I'm going to tell it like it is.*
> *I hope you can take it like it is.*
> — Malcolm X

ASKING FOR PERMISSION TO SHARE

Although it's taken for granted, given the nature of a coaching relationship, that the coach has permission to share their thinking with their clients, there are occasions when it's useful to outright ask for permission. This prepares your client for what they're about to hear, and gives you an opportunity to preface your statement, which is particularly appropriate if it's going to be hard to hear or it will have a major impact. If for any reason they say they don't want to hear it, you have to move on. Whether or not you're right is irrelevant; it's all about the data you cull from the response.

* * *

Amy reported that she and her husband had a huge fight that morning, saying, "I just know it means we are going to get divorced." Her coach asked for permission: "As I heard that, something came up for me and I want to know if it's okay to share." After Amy said yes, and the coach said, "It sounds to me as though that's the same as saying 'I took one piece of cake; now I'll become obese.' What do you think when you hear that?"

An exaggerated metaphor immediately helps your client become aware of faulty thinking. If they're hesitant, resistant, talk rapidly, sound bored, or give away too much detail all the time, and you sense something else going on underneath any of those behaviors, it's *vital* to share your thoughts: "I'm finding that there is so much detail that I'm having trouble following, and [I wonder where else in your life this might be showing up] or [what do you think that's about?]"

SPINNING STORIES

As human beings, our tendency is to think the worst. If we make up a story, we ruminate and create a downward spiral of negativity instead of being optimistic. Our minds are so powerful that we can make up stories about anything and everything without seeing the bigger picture objectively and distinguishing what's real from what isn't. What coaching offers clients is an opportunity to identify their faulty conclusions through direct communication.

* * *

Marcia's boss called her at the end of the work day and told her that he had something really important to talk about with her, but that it would have to wait until the next day when he would see her in person. He stressed it was something he was not willing to share over the phone. That's when she began to spin stories. She thought that she had perhaps done something very wrong, or he was going to leave the company and she would lose her job, or worse yet, he was going to fire her. It turned out he was getting a divorce and it had nothing to do with her. [*Taking It Personally* theme]

* * *

Jordan had been friends with Matt since boyhood. Now they were in their late twenties and Jordan was concerned that Matt was partying like a teen instead of acting like an adult. Yet he worried that if he said what he was really thinking, he would lose his best friend.

The coach's role is to help him see that he is drawing a conclusion that may or may not be true. She might ask, "What if you found out that instead of losing your friend, Matt would appreciate your honesty and gain more respect for you? What would that mean for you?" While Jordan might or might not lose Matt's friendship by sharing his concern, this question at least stops Jordan from thinking in only one direction. Another option is to point out that if Jordan and Matt are in fact growing apart, maybe Jordan has already lost his best friend. What might be true about that?

A question I often ask myself in situations such as Jordan's is, "What is true in this moment?" It works well, because the truth is I don't know anything but the facts.

50/50 CHANCES

When you hear a faulty conclusion drawn by your client, such as, "I need it to be perfect!" or, "I know I will make the wrong choice," you can offer them the opposite as a possibility instead of trying to convince them otherwise.

There's a 50/50 chance that things will go the opposite way, and neither you nor your client will know ahead of time. It would sound like, "What if there is no wrong choice, what would that be like?" What you're doing is opening up your client to seeing their situation more objectively and, consequently, you provide relief in the moment. You're helping them realize that, because something could go either way, focusing only on the negative makes no sense. That said, I often include that there is a chance it could go either way and ask what they are willing to do.

Direct communication relies heavily on the delivery of your message. Especially when the mind chatter kicks in, it's time to share what's coming up for you. *How* you do that makes all the difference. Keep in mind that removing the word *you* although tricky at first, allows the client to hear what you are noticing without feeling defensive. Another good reminder is that clients (all people) spin stories without necessarily knowing the facts. Reminding the client of what is true in the moment curtails the spinning and puts things in perspective.

DEFENSES

A defense shows up in a coaching conversation as a specific behavior to avoid something, like a barrier. A defense can be used to avoid a painful topic. In general, it's an avoidance tactic, such as humor to mask pain. If you notice a defensive behavior, it's worth exploring because it indicates there's likely a challenge in other areas of your client's life as well. Below are common types of defenses and how to address them:

Data-dumping

Clients often give us far more detail than we need. It doesn't necessarily mean that they're avoiding something. However, there may be times when your client provides far too much detail and information to avoid sharing the real problem or the real truth.

When you reflect on what you've heard and ask a question that would normally move the conversation forward, and your client continues to provide more detail, it *might* indicate defensive data-dumping; they might be avoiding what they really want to tell you, or perhaps they're afraid to tell you. It's your role to monitor the intention behind the details because they might simply have a strong need to share them or think that you won't understand if they don't provide every detail.

Emotional state

There are times when clients become emotional during a coaching session. Sometimes it's upset and crying, other times it might be anger or frustration. When they're upset or tearful, allow them the space they need to let their emotions out. *Wait until they speak again before asking your next question.* They might say, "Sorry that I got so upset," or "I didn't expect that." Then a question (as previously mentioned) such as "What is making this so emotional for you?" forces them to immediately shift their state of mind. Stay in the objective-listener role and monitor the context and intention behind the emotion. Most often, it's genuine, but it could be an avoidance tactic.

Confusion and avoidance

When your client appears to be confused or expresses things in a confusing way, get clarification before proceeding. However, it's also possible that the confusion is simply avoidance and an unwillingness to share what's really true. This defense manifests when they're not willing to face or do something they know deep down would be in their best interest.

Attacking or blaming you

Although it's uncommon, there may be times when a client attacks or blames you as the coach for something not going right. More often than not, it's misplaced anger, and it's crucial to remain neutral and unattached. By asking open questions, you will likely discover what is really going on.

Submission

While this does not occur often, sometimes a client wants to be compliant and please the coach. You might notice a great deal of agreement and/or lack of push-back. They might continually agree with everything you say, or always tell you they're fine even though circumstances indicate otherwise. This defense could be an important pattern in their life, so it needs to be pointed out and addressed.

QUESTIONS FOR REFLECTION

- What fears do you have about using truly direct communication?
- What could you say that would be more direct than, "I wonder if you are getting a little upset with your wife when she maxes out your credit cards?"
- What changes might direct communication create in your coaching practice?
- What might be helpful when your client is spinning a story and you don't want to get trapped by their imagination?

CHAPTER 13

ADVANCED COACHING TECHNIQUES

It's still magic, even if you know how it's done.
— Terry Pratchett

You already know that a coach should spend the majority of their time listening instead of speaking. However, the words you *do* say are extremely important to your client's progress and your relationship. While I'm not a fan of coaching scripts or formulas, in this chapter you will discover some communication guidelines that will help you speak with your client in a way that fosters their growth and self-awareness. You will also discover that clients often employ or end up with short-term strategies that substitute for a change in thinking that would otherwise support progress long term.

PAINTING THE PICTURE

Painting the picture is about putting your client literally *into* a situation in their mind as though it's occurring right now rather than imagining it at a later time.

Coaches often ask, "What do you envision for yourself in [one year / five years / ten years]?" The client's response to this question is total supposition and guesswork. It doesn't provide relevant data other than what they *hope* for. In contrast, painting a vivid picture with some distinct and realistic details elicits a visceral response. *It can even get "thinkers" to feel.*

You can do this using either an upside or downside scenario. People often believe they want something without having considered the drawbacks. For example, nine-to-five workers wish they could make their own hours and not have to be somewhere every day. They might not have considered what it means to be at home every day, to not have a steady paycheck, to have to constantly elicit new business, and to work far more hours because their office is "right there."

* * *

Chelsea, a young single mother, really wanted to be in a relationship. She was living in a basement apartment and was very embarrassed about her living conditions. She always avoided having people come to her house.

To paint a picture for her, I asked, "Let's suppose tomorrow morning your doorbell rings, you open the door, and there stands the man of your dreams. He has a great sense of humor, he loves children, he's intelligent, he has a great job [all the things she said she wanted]. What do you do?"

Chelsea paused, gasped, and said, "I can't invite him in." I said, "Okay, then what does that mean for you?" She replied, "I guess what it means is I'm really not as ready as I thought I was for a relationship."

Just putting her in the situation as though it was actually happening prompted a major revelation for Chelsea. When you do this, clients almost always have a visceral response, because if you do it well, they're picturing themselves literally in that place and a feeling arises.

* * *

Monica told me she had wanted to create a home office for a whole year and yet it hadn't happened. I asked her what she thought might be the reason. She then explained that it was her daughter's playroom and she felt guilty about replacing it.

I painted the picture, and everything shifted. I asked, "What would it be like if your home office is all set up, the furniture is in place, the walls are painted the color you want, pictures are hung, and it just looks really great? What would that mean?"

That's when she realized that she only needed a portion of the room as her office and could leave the rest as a playroom, and she couldn't wait to set it up. Within a short time, she had a functioning office.

When you can paint a vivid picture as if it's something already in place, your client can respond to the emotion it brings up. This works more effectively than putting them in a future scenario.

* * *

Sherry was unhappy and felt as though her life was off-kilter. We looked at the three main facets that were contributing to the problem: home, job, and friends. She wasn't sure if one, two, or all of them had to change, and if so, which one should be first.

For no particular reason, I started painting a picture about changing her job and kept all of the other variables as is. I described a new job that she would love, with a lot more money, great people, and a great commute, and included that she would have the exact same friends and live in the exact same place. When I asked, "What about this works for you?" her response was that it still didn't feel right.

Then we looked at changing her friends: "Presume you have the same job as now, live in the same place, and have new groups of friends with whom you feel comfortable and supported, and who are usually available. What about this works for you?" Sherry responded that it still didn't feel right.

Next, I painted a picture in which she kept the same job and friends but was now living in a completely different neighborhood with lots of restaurants, stores that stayed open late, and lots of activity. She immediately knew that was the thing that had to change first. If I had created the pictures in a different order, the answer would likely have come a lot sooner.

REMOVING THE OBSTACLE

When something seems to be an obstacle, such as, "If only I had [more time / more money / more space / etc.]," asking what things would be like without that factor (or excuse) can show your client in a moment what they really want: "Suppose you had all the [time/money/space/etc.] in the world. What would you do?" And it's even more effective to paint the picture as well, such as: "Let's suppose you won the lottery and you had all the money in the world. What would you do?"

This concept is important because it helps your client discern not what they *think* they want, not what they *should* want, not what's feasible, but what would be ideal. This helps them see *possibilities* first, then look at what's realistic. And if it's not realistic, perhaps there's a version of the picture that is, or maybe there's a way to get what they want going down a path that they haven't even imagined yet.

That's called *removing the obstacle*. Question what is perceived to be in the way as though it most likely isn't. And if it is in the way (such as money), look for a realistic alternative to the ideal.

LET YOUR CLIENT KNOW THEY HAVE A CHOICE

Your client's dilemma often comes down to *choice*. They have the choice to let it go or hold on to it. Knowing they have a choice can often be the most important thing they need to hear.

While this sounds like such a simple concept, it can be extremely powerful. Clients often feel as though they have to surrender, or that they're relegated to something, when in fact they have a choice. The choice may be one that they don't like, but the important thing is that there is one.

How many times have you heard someone complain about their job, their boss, their spouse, or their environment? And how many times have you thought, "Why don't they change it?" We tend to believe that if something doesn't meet our expectations or isn't the way we want it to be, it has to remain that way. It's as if we have to accept it, and the only thing we can do about it is complain.

* * *

Richard was lamenting about the unhealthy food offered at his workplace cafeteria: "Why can't they serve healthier food? Don't they realize this is bad nutrition?" I immediately thought of three viable options: bring your own lunch; speak to the person in charge of the food choices; or go out to lunch.

Of course, rather than share those thoughts I asked, "What might be something you can do to affect a difference?" or "What might be some options that could work for you?"

One of my favorite questions that I often ask myself: "What would a wise person do?" This is an exceptionally thought-provoking question regardless of the circumstance, because it takes people out of their ego and overthinking. The answer is often something we haven't yet thought of, or it gives us permission to do something we hadn't thought possible. We always have options and choices, but we get locked into "this is how it is" thinking and are blind to the possibilities.

There's *always* a choice. If someone just refuses to see that that's the case, I like to say, "I can hear that you believe that there's absolutely no choice. In that case, what would you like to do?" This begs the question of whether they're willing to make a change or prefer to accept what is.

* * *

Abby said, "I'm in this awful marriage. He's so mean and he's petty. He's inconsiderate. I could've walked out at any moment, but I have to put up with him because it's better than being alone with two small children. I couldn't survive, and I'll never be okay if I leave. I'll have no money."

Does Abby have a choice? Absolutely. She might not be comfortable with any of the options, but it's helpful for her to accept that there are alternatives, whether she chooses them or not. It's also helpful for her to recognize that she is in fact making a choice by staying in the awful marriage.

Focusing on choice helps people see that their choice may be an interpretation in their mind, and they're not as stuck as they thought they were.

* * *

Charles, a director at a large firm, was frustrated by a colleague not holding his direct reports accountable for completing work on time. He firmly believed in holding people accountable and wanted a way to address the situation with his colleague.

Charles followed up his story by saying, "I feel like I have to say something to him," so I asked him, "What makes you think that you *have* to say something to your colleague?" After a long pause, Charles realized that he had taken it upon himself to change his colleague's behavior. Hearing this question made him realize that he had a *choice* whether or not to address the issue, not an obligation. Acknowledging this choice freed Charles from

214

taking on his colleague's situation. He was then able to let it go and focus on his own challenges at work instead.

Let your client know that they have a choice to let go of (or hold on to) an idea. It gives them power and agency over their situation.

TELLING VERSUS LETTING YOUR CLIENT FIGURE IT OUT

In coaching, we're taught to never tell our client anything, but to let them figure it out. However, there are exceptions to this rule that are perfectly appropriate, so we avoid frustrating them.

When you know something for a fact, it makes sense to share it with your client. A classic example is when they confuse self-care with being selfish. You can ask how they define each one, but you can also provide a clear distinction and ask what they'll do regarding that distinction going forward. Offering distinctions can be particularly helpful, such as the distinction between *forgive* and *forget*.

As an outside, objective listener, when you perceive or observe something going on with your client, it is crucial to share it. There's no need to make your client figure out something that is obvious to you. Share what you surmise, followed by a simple check-in question, and allow them to respond. This is an opportunity for direct communication.

Suppose you're working with a client who wants to quit his job before looking for a new one. It's appropriate to tell him (fact) that it's easier to find a new job when you already have one.

On the other hand, suppose you're working with Janice, who is consistently late for appointments and always chooses to blame something or somebody else. You might be tempted to tell her that if she would just leave enough time it wouldn't be a problem. However, in a case like this, you want to help her see that she must take responsibility for her lateness and that blaming isn't appropriate. This is when it's all about your client and how she thinks and behaves. Then your role is to help *her* become more self-aware.

NO CONSEQUENCES: PRESENTING AN OPTION TO ENCOURAGE YOUR CLIENT TO EXPRESS THEMSELVES FREELY

Your client might indicate that they're afraid of facing, confronting, or challenging another person. A thought-provoking question you can ask is "What would you say (or do) if there were no consequences or repercussions?" This allows them to literally speak what is on their mind. Then you can extrapolate the overall sentiment and message and ask them to find a way to share the message so that the other person can hear it.

*   *   *

Daniel was complaining about his wife's "passionate" feedback. When I asked him what he really wanted to say if there were no consequences, he replied, "I'm so tired of you yelling at me. When you talk that way, I just shut down. Why do you always have to yell at your family instead of speaking in a friendly and calm tone of voice?" Then I asked him how he might share his thoughts in a way that his wife could hear them. Daniel replied, "If you want me to hear you, it would be helpful if you could dial down your tone and speak in a way that doesn't sound like you are talking 'at' me and being judgmental, but rather being curious and open. That way you'll have a greater impact."

LISTEN for the 1%

In coaching we're always looking for our client's strengths. Often, they already know what's working well for them.

A very common mistake is when we don't focus on the 1 percent that's not working. When your client says, "I've almost got it!" you can ask, "What about the part you don't have?" That's where the coaching is. "Almost" is an indicator: "I'm just about fine." You can ask, "Well it sounds like you're not totally fine, so what would make the difference?"

It's important to validate and tell people what a great job they've done, but the way you can help someone is to focus on the part that's not totally okay. The help is in the small portion that's not working. When you hear, "Well, I'm ninety-nine percent sure," the logical question should be "What would make it one hundred percent?" You want to find out exactly where the coaching needs to happen.

To determine how close or far someone is from what they want, coaches often use the "1 to 10 scale" to find out where their client is in a particular process. This data might seem helpful for the coach, but it can be more revealing to ask where they are on a *spectrum* because it evokes a more detailed and personalized response. It paints a picture of how they feel versus categorizing how they feel.

For example, if you ask, "On a scale of one to ten, what is your commitment to learning Spanish?" and your client responds, "Eight," this doesn't reveal what is needed to help them be fully committed. If you feel compelled to use this scale, find out what's missing that would make it a 10.

That said, a more useful question might be, "What is your commitment to learning Spanish?" Your client might respond, "I've thought about it for many years and now I realize that it will help me at my job as well as when I travel. Therefore, I'm now enrolling in a language program and I'm excited to get started." By asking this as an open question, your client can respond in whatever way they choose, and you will get helpful data.

METAPHORS

One easy way to share directly is to use a metaphor or create a visual image that immediately lets your client know how you interpret something they said. Whether it's a metaphor, simile, or analogy, they are equally effective.

The key is that your words come from your *observation*, not your personal viewpoint. When you objectively observe how your client's information is coming across, there is no right or wrong or potential for attaching to the result. They can tell you whether they find your observation accurate, surprising, or totally off base. The important thing is that you share what you observe. Often a metaphor that captures the concept expressed by your client can create immediate awareness.

Metaphors are extremely powerful and can immediately bring something to light without any detrimental effect. If your client says something contradictory, avoidant, or that has a mixed message, a metaphor is a useful way to reveal how you are observing this. And there are tricks and tips for creating metaphors that can make it easier for you. (Keep in mind that if your client uses a metaphor, it's your responsibility to continue it.)

> *The most important aspect of creating a metaphor is to first figure out the concept or the overall gist of what you're surmising.*

Since the metaphor is your observation, express it using third person so the client can hear it objectively. This means not saying, for instance, "It's as if you were to..." but rather, "It's as if *someone* were to...."

Over time you'll develop your own metaphors for the primary themes you encounter in your coaching. Feel free to employ the examples of metaphors in the themes chapter or any provided below as you see fit and use them as a springboard to create your own.

In retrospect, I noticed when I first began creating metaphors, they all involved water — a pool, a lake, the ocean, a boat, sailing, etc. I didn't plan it that way; it just seemed to happen. To make it easier to learn how to create them, think of a topic that's very familiar to you, such as gardening, baking, cars, cooking, horses, running, etc. By using a familiar topic, you'll be able to create metaphors that feel authentic.

> *When you present a metaphor, it is absolutely imperative that you ask a follow-up question to check it out with your client.*

Each of the following examples includes a coaching situation, a related concept, a metaphor, *and the follow-up question* that invites your client to consider what you've shared and let you know their thoughts.

Situation: A client is seeking validation from his father. He kept going to him to feel better about work and stress and complained because his father always said, "Keep going," and not much else. He became frustrated and resentful that he wasn't getting the validation he wanted.

Concept: Wants something he can't get from that person

Metaphor: It seems like a person who keeps going to the hardware store for milk. What comes to mind?

Situation: A client, who is a new coach, complained that she spends a great deal of time with prospective clients and then finds out they can't pay her fees.

Concept: Neglecting to screen prospects

Metaphor: This sounds like a salesperson working at a high-end department store, and a disheveled bag lady comes in browsing for clothing, and the salesperson spends considerable time trying to help her even though it seems obvious that she can't afford to buy anything. What do you think?

Situation: A client claims that he wants to lose weight, but he keeps his house stocked with junk food.

Concept: Conflicting priorities

Metaphor: It sounds like a person who wants to run a marathon but never does any training. What do you think?

Situation: A client keeps talking about going to Hawaii for a vacation, going through brochures, and studying information on the internet, but definitely does not have the finances to vacation there.

Concept: Wants something even though it's not realistic

Metaphor: It's like a vegetarian who goes to a steakhouse and studies the menu even though there is nothing on the menu they can eat. What comes up when you hear that?

Situation: A client is having problems at work. She says, "My boss is sexually harassing me. Whenever I walk by, he either winks at me or tries to grab me. It's embarrassing and uncomfortable." Later she reveals that she accepts his dinner invitations each week.

Concept: Mixed messages

Metaphor: This sounds like a person who wants to live on a monthly budget but then goes out and buys a new car. How does that come across?

Situation: Your client gets really excited talking about retirement. Finally, he'll be able to spend time with his grandchildren and not have to get up so early in the morning. Yet he keeps taking on long-term contract work, complaining that work is so busy, and saying they need him because of his expertise.

Concept: Contradiction

Metaphor: This sounds like a person who wants to do well on her final exam, and then goes out and gets drunk the night before the test. What do you think hearing that?

Situation: A client shares about a huge deadline pending at work. It's a major project and will influence future business, and they're counting on it going well. Then she discloses that she plays games on the internet at work at every opportunity and takes especially long lunches.

Concept: Avoidance

Metaphor: This sounds like a person who desperately wants to be in a relationship but rarely leaves the house and doesn't join any online dating sites. What does that sound like?

I encourage you to experiment with metaphors! They're powerful and can be fun to create once you realize it's about first getting the gist or concept and using a topic that's familiar to you. Although it takes practice, in truth you probably already use several metaphors, such as "When it rains, it pours."

STRATEGIES

As humans, we create strategies for dealing with life. They can be advantageous, but they can also be harmful.

> *It's the* intention *behind a strategy that determines how it affects us.*

If your intention is to make a plan, grow, evolve, move past your fears, or become more secure, it's helpful to devise a strategy such as establishing a regular meditation practice. If you use a strategy to avoid, escape, compensate, or distract, such as blaming others or denial, it won't result in what is really wanted — love, connection, or acceptance — because the intention is not healthy.

Ramona had fantasy relationships and continually "fell in love" with movie stars and athletes. She did this because she didn't believe she was worthy of a genuine relationship and was too afraid of rejection to pursue one.

People are often not aware that they have devised a strategy to cope with getting something they want. Such a strategy works only in the short term until the person becomes too unhappy or feels unfulfilled.

Sue was a high-achieving top executive at a major law firm. In her personal life, she let men control her because she thought that if she showed her power, they would feel threatened and leave the relationship.

You can help your client become aware of their temporary strategy and then find a healthy way to get their desires met. Consider this one: "I want to lose weight, so I will never eat chocolate cake or French fries again." What are the chances that such will power will prevail over a lifetime? Because it doesn't address the underlying challenge, such as creating a different self-image or a different relationship with food, it's only temporary. The underlying reasons for overeating or for wanting to lose weight have not been faced, such as overeating because she thinks her husband is having an affair or wanting to be thin so she will find someone for a relationship.

In coaching you'll hear strategies in phrases like, "I just have to remember" and, "I will just have to stop doing this." Those are clues that your client is relying on will power and any improvement will be temporary; they're not creating a new way of thinking.

Coaches are not immune to creating strategies either. You've probably heard other coaches talk about waiting to launch their coaching practice until they take additional courses or have the perfect logo, business card, or website designed. These are just strategies to avoid something they fear, and they are deeply rooted in beliefs such as, "I'm not capable" or perhaps, "I really don't want to do this." Instead of being honest with themselves, they create a strategy to justify their behavior.

* * *

Kevin lived with major clutter, particularly in his office and on his desk. Rather than addressing how to deal with the mess, we looked into the reason that the mess was there in the first place. It turned out that it was his way of avoiding the success that his family was pressuring him toward! He had invented a strategy that justified his failure. Once he understood his strategy, he was able to move forward.

* * *

Steve wanted to feel powerful and have people like him, so he went out of his way to buy expensive gifts and show up at every event, funeral, and meeting even if it didn't suit his schedule. He became a martyr who created indebtedness from others believing that made him powerful and well-liked. Instead, he gave up his authenticity.

Below are many of the common strategies with unhealthy intentions. It's not important to learn their names. What is important is to recognize them, point them out as unhealthy behaviors, and help clients find healthy ways to get what they want.

Put-downs

Someone who uses put-downs as a strategy might think, "I'm going to make you feel crappy so that I feel good. I'm going to dismiss what you have to say so that I look like I'm the one who has the good answers."

Withdrawals

It's just as much a strategy for someone to take a back seat when in a group of people as it is to put themselves in the lead position. People who stay very quiet sometimes do so to avoid the feeling of rejection, or they fear meeting new people and not knowing what to say.

Protection

When someone wants to shield or protect another person, it can get in the way of their own well-being. Someone might get a bad health diagnosis and decide not to tell their spouse because they don't believe their spouse will be able to handle it and will be too upset.

Projection

This is when a person makes it seem as though someone else feels the same way they do. If they're devastated about a breakup and, at the same time, one of their friends' relationships ends, they act as though they, too, are devastated, even if that's not the case.

Compensation

This is when someone attempts to balance another person's behavior by going to the other extreme. For example, when one parent is very strict, the other becomes too lenient.

Will power

This is when someone deliberately decides to do something or refrains from doing something in the hope that their efforts will last, such as diet, exercise, or stopping all TV.

Denial

Someone is in denial when they believe on a conscious level that something isn't the way it really is. For example, they suspect their spouse is cheating yet choose to believe their spouse's excuses. Their subconscious intention is to numb their pain and not face the truth. Thus, the expression, "The spouse is the last person to know."

On the other hand, denial can be a blessing, especially after a death or traumatic event. When the pain is just too great, we use denial as a way to get through it until it eventually registers both consciously and subconsciously. In some extreme cases people may remain in denial indefinitely.

Displaced anger

Displaced anger shows up as taking anger or frustration out on someone nearby rather than on the source of the anger. For example, in a triangular relationship, the wife wants to take out her anger on the "other woman" rather than face her husband and their relationship.

Lying

People lie or embellish the truth to avoid facing or admitting the actual truth, because they're afraid of the truth, to look more important, or to compensate for low self-esteem.

Blaming others

It's a classic strategy to blame someone else for our shortcomings: "It was [the traffic / the rain / the crowds] that made me late." In other words, not taking responsibility.

Addictions

When people get addicted to something, whether it's gambling, sex, alcohol, or even a relationship, it's to avoid dealing with feelings or facing something.

People-pleasing

This one has come up several times already in *The HeART of Laser-Focused Coaching*, as it's also a coaching theme. It's a person's tendency to confuse caring for others with taking care of them. It also manifests as giving more than receiving for fear of losing another person's love. The need to feel important is so strong that someone goes to all lengths to get it fulfilled by other people because they can't value themselves.

Sacrificing oneself

This includes being a martyr or not asserting oneself. In this strategy, someone gives up what they really want to make others happy or because they fear being judged poorly. They choose suffering instead of speaking up or living their life on their own terms.

Gossiping

Gossiping is often an attempt to create a bond with someone by demeaning someone else. If two people feel as though they are aligned against others, they believe they are closer to each other and/or superior to others.

Overeating and undereating

Overeating and undereating are ways a person can feel in control when they don't have control over other areas of their life.

Obsession

Spending an inordinate amount of time on something like sports, political causes, committees, or religious activities can be a way to avoid core issues in one's own life rather than addressing and handling them.

Being overly busy

People employ this strategy because they believe it makes others think they are important or successful. Someone who is overly busy is likely compensating for a feeling of inadequacy or not facing that their life is out of order. This strategy falls apart when the person gets burned out.

It behooves you to take the time to find out *why* your client is asking to make changes in their life. Your job is to explore and discover what's really needed and help to change the perspective rather than devise a temporary strategy that simply alleviates their symptoms — the band-aid approach. When your client says something like "I'll put a sticky note on my mirror to remind me each day," it's a classic example of a temporary strategy, because after a period of time it will be ignored. Using stickies and calendars is okay as long as doing so accompanies a real shift in your client's thinking.

* * *

Maria, a new coach, said, "I have a client who is very clingy, whiny, and gets very attached. She seems to glom onto people like Velcro. I'm thinking that I should do an exercise with her that we learned in coaching school and recommend an appropriate book as a strategy."

Although the exercise or the book might be helpful, it is more helpful for Maria's client to discover the underlying problem that needs to be addressed. It's likely this client has unmet needs. Together with her client, Maria must figure out what the need is (attention, acceptance, etc.) that's not being met and what's driving this behavior. That way, Maria can help her find ways to get the need met so she can experience a permanent change in behavior.

While it's important to have some healthy strategies to deal with life's challenges, in my experience it's far more important to discover what's causing the problem in the first place. Unhealthy strategies only work for so long. They can "fix" a problem in the short term, but they don't help when the problem (or a similar one) arises in the future. Once the root cause is exposed for someone feeling stuck, a true shift occurs, and they can't go back to their original thinking.

> *A strategy* along *with a change in thinking can work well. The problem is when a strategy (such as only a sticky note) substitutes for a change in thinking.*

Becoming aware of strategies and defenses and listening for the intention behind them can make a huge difference in helping someone continue their progress or become aware of how the strategy is working against them. The magic happens when you provide the time and space for a client to understand the reasons behind their strategies and defenses. Most people never consider this, so you're providing a deeply valuable experience for your client when you facilitate that exploration.

Now that you may have some new techniques and awareness around different ways to help clients, I hope you will experiment and try them out and notice what works.

QUESTIONS FOR REFLECTION

- What comes to mind when you consider focusing on the 1 percent that is not working for your client?
- What might change in your coaching if you paint the picture rather than question the future?
- What topic or hobby might help you create metaphors?
- What might change in your coaching now that you can recognize temporary strategies or defenses your client might be employing? What strategies, if any, do you use regularly and what might help you find a healthy way to get what you want?

CHAPTER 14

COACHING CHALLENGES

We don't grow when things are easy; we grow when we face challenges.
— Unknown

Since we are working with human beings, there are challenges that arise when coaching. Some of them keep you from staying focused on your client, others exist because both you and your client have a similar struggle, and sometimes, the line between therapy and coaching isn't as clear cut as we believe. There are occasions when it's difficult to know what to ask next. Actually, there's a very simple solution so keep reading.

STAYING OUT OF THERAPY

Some coaches might struggle with the distinction between therapy and coaching. There are many types of therapy and some overlap with coaching. However, in coaching, we want our relationship to be collaborative in that we work in partnership with our client to find the best results. This is a distinction from the therapeutic relationship. In traditional therapy, the therapist is the expert and the client is the one who needs help. In coaching we walk the path together.

Therapy is predominantly designed to heal someone, whereas coaching is about personal and/or professional growth allowing the client to reach their potential. Coaching can be purely professionally based, addressing topics such as leadership skills and business development as well as personal challenges.

Therapy is generally a longer process. Coaching is meant to efficiently get to the heart of the matter and support forward movement. As coaches, we are often taught to scrupulously avoid going back in time. Yet, identifying the source of their challenge can be very beneficial as long as you are careful not to focus too much on emotional content and cross over into therapy.

It's a balance. Your client's feelings are important, because in the majority of coaching conversations, the goal is to see a change in their perspective as well as the underlying emotion (fear, confusion, lack of clarity, anger, doubt, etc.). The real change, despite the words and thinking, is actually changing the emotion underlying the words. In the beginning of a coaching conversation, it's helpful to ascertain whether your client is frustrated, confused, upset, angry, etc. By the end of that conversation, hopefully they feel differently.

I encourage you to *dip* into feelings in your coaching conversations, but then quickly emerge from that and *immediately* focus on the present. For example, "I hear that your father had unusually high expectations of you when you were a child, but now, as an adult, what could be different?"

Here's an example of how to explore the source of a problem without crossing a boundary into therapy:

Alice: I've had this problem forever. I can't seem to get past it.

Coach: When was the first time you noticed it?

Alice: I remember a nun who was my teacher in third grade who made me feel so ashamed.

Coach: Where is that nun now?

Alice: Oh, I'm sure she's long gone; she was old back then.

Coach: It seems as though that nun is still very much alive in your mind today. What do you think?

Here's an example of using the same concept for a different situation:

* * *

Robert, an accomplished physicist who earned a PhD, authored several books, and heads a company, lamented that he "should" have been doing more than he was. He said, "My second-grade teacher told me I can do more than I think I can." And I said, "I'm guessing there's no way that your teacher, if alive, would ever remember saying that, so what choice, now as an adult, could you make regarding how you view all of your accomplishments?"

As I mentioned earlier, should emotions surface, it's important to allow space for the client to feel them. However, you don't want them to stay in that emotional state for a significant amount of time because that's not where we function as coaches. No matter how uncomfortable, wait for them to signal that they are ready to proceed. A question that would then get them to think and come out of the emotional state might be, "What is making this so emotional for you?"

Therapy might be more appropriate if your client has deeply rooted trauma or:

- Consistently fails to follow through with agreements or assignments
- Mentions suicide or staying home all day and not being productive at all
- Seems extremely stuck and resistant
- Has deep-rooted, unresolved problems from their youth that are affecting their adult life
- Wants help with a diagnosed illness such as depression, anorexia, or anxiety

That said, a client with any of the above issues who comes to coaching because they are stuck in some other aspect of their life can do coaching and therapy simultaneously. All of us have issues and all of us have traumas. The difference between therapy-appropriate issues and coaching-appropriate issues is how the client is managing them in the moment and whether these are bumps in the road or are deeply embedded, preventing forward movement.

For example:

* * *

Belinda, thirty-seven years old, had been dating for many years and really wanted to settle down, get married, and start a family. She had shared early on that she lost her father at a very young age. While we also focused on job-related challenges, her progress in the dating arena wasn't going well, so we discussed the possibility of her going to therapy simultaneously. She went ahead with that plan. After completing about eight months of therapy dealing with her traumatic experience at a young age, she stayed on with the coaching. Soon after, she met her husband, and they started a family.

LOSING FOCUS ON YOUR CLIENT

Many coaches identify with their clients because they've experienced a similar situation or because they pick up on their client's emotion and start to feel it. If you ever feel stressed during or after a coaching session, you might be unconsciously falling into this trap.

* * *

Lizbeth, a soft-spoken coach from the southern part of the United States, had a client from New York who worried her. She always wondered if he was angry with her or planned to stop being coached by her. When we explored the situation, she realized that she was not accustomed to his brusque and rapid New York communication style. Her client was, in fact, very pleased with Lizbeth's coaching; he just spoke in a way that was unfamiliar to her.

Even though you might think it's about you, it's never about you. You might be the impetus or the trigger for an emotion your client is feeling, but that doesn't make it about you.

Use this knowledge in your coaching sessions to avoid taking on your client's emotions or taking things personally if you believe they're angry or frustrated with you. No matter what you have or haven't done, they have specific needs (to be on time, to avoid interruptions, to look smart). Everything in the coaching sessions is about them and their need.

Even if your client says something critical or expresses a powerful emotion to you as their coach, it's their emotion, even if it seems as though they're making it about you. It's an important coaching skill to be able to see your client as they are and let them express their emotions without taking it personally.

I had a client who was angry and yelling, not only about his situation but also at me. He felt that what happened was my fault. I remained completely neutral and questioned him as to what the anger was really about. It had absolutely nothing to do with me. I was simply the person available to lash out against. It's important to not get emotionally invested and maintain neutrality so that you can be the objective coach you are meant to be.

MISSING RELEVANT PATTERNS

What clients do with you, they do in the outside world. And what they do in the outside world, they do with you. When your client says, "You know I had this job, but I really couldn't stay. My boss was so horrendous I just had to leave. And then I got this other job. You know I really liked the work, but my co-workers were so competitive I had to leave that one. And then I got this other job...."

Guess what? They're going to respond the same way to you, and it won't be long before they leave you too! If, however, you step back and uncover their pattern of always finding a problem and moving on, you'll get to the heart of their issue and truly transform their pattern. Your client will unknowingly tell you early on what their basic pattern is, which is why it's so important to sit back, observe, and listen for the deeper story.

GETTING SEDUCED BY THE "OTHER" PERSON

One of the biggest traps we can fall into is listening more intently to the other person in our client's story (spouse, boss, friend, etc.) than to our client. This is because it's often the other person who creates the excitement and conflict in the story. It's the other person who generates the emotion in the storyteller. We get curious about the details, either because we're nosey, we want to validate the emotions the storyteller is experiencing, or the story triggers a personal memory.

* * *

Tom began his coaching session with, "I'm so frustrated. My wife is always on my case about not putting my clothes away. I'm tired of her complaints." His coach asked, "What do you want her to do when she isn't pleased?"

The coaching conversation began to derail from there because the focus was now on his wife instead of Tom. His wife can't be helped or changed in this conversation; the only thing his coach can do is help Tom with how he views and copes with the situation. No matter how you look at it, Tom needs assistance. Maybe his wife could address it differently, but we aren't in conversation with her, are we? Focus on your client, not the "other."

SHARED BELIEF SYNDROME — IDENTIFYING WITH YOUR CLIENT

As human beings with ideas about what life "should" be like, we share many of the same beliefs as our clients. It is important to allow that awareness to keep us from missing coaching opportunities. You often encounter a limiting belief, thought, or idea shared between you and your client. This shared idea is transparent and seems natural and true for both of you. And when both of you share a similar idea or value, it's difficult to be objective.

The problem is it's hard to realize when you share a limiting belief with your client because it's invisible. The first clue is when you realize you agree with your client. If they say, "It was very challenging," and you think, *"Yes, that was very challenging,"* the two of you share similar thoughts about the situation, and you can miss an opportunity to question this.

A coach who doesn't see the situation as challenging would be quick to question, "What makes it so difficult?" Therefore, the moment you notice you're agreeing with your client, it's time to step back and act *as if* you have no idea what they're talking about — as though it's new information. This is one way to remain truly curious.

The concept of *shared belief syndrome* is important because no two people come to the same conclusion in exactly the same way. Conclusions are, by nature, drawn from experience and history, unique to each individual. To understand your client, get curious as to *how the belief was established.* You know what made something difficult for you, but what you want to know is what made it difficult for *them.* This opens up further avenues of reflection, discovery, and action.

It's uncanny, but whatever you're working on in your life is going to show up in your client's life. When it does, you want to be able to be objective. Look at how *shared belief syndrome* is present in each of the following situations:

- Your client believes the best way to get a promotion is by putting in overtime. If you just nod and agree, you miss an opportunity for coaching. Another coach would be curious and explore other options since there is more than one path to getting promoted.
- A twice-divorced female coach has a female client who wants a relationship, and the coach and the client both believe that men are not trustworthy. There is little possibility for coaching in this situation, but if the coach steps back and

acts as if she doesn't understand her client's mistrust of men, she can be truly curious.

- A client is looking for a new job in a bad economy, and both the coach and the client think it's almost impossible to find one. This is a missed opportunity for coaching. Another coach might think that while the job hunt might not be easy, it isn't impossible, and would encourage the client to keep looking or explore creative ways to maximize their efforts.

As soon as you notice that you agree with your client, it's time to take a step back and *act as if* you don't understand. You can say, "That's an interesting statement," and then question their assertion. Assume nothing is true. Step back as if it were brand new information that you have never heard before. Another coach would just ask and be curious because it doesn't make sense. While you might agree with the belief, you definitely did not arrive at your belief in the same way your client did, so it behooves you to always remain curious and skeptical so you can uncover the underlying assumptions guiding them. This provides an opportunity for your client to learn more about themselves.

WHEN YOUR CLIENT ASKS YOU OR THEMSELVES A QUESTION

Occasionally a client will ask, "What would you do in this case?" Your tendency might be to simply tell them, but keep in mind that what works for you might not work for someone else.

The problem is your client might get frustrated because they really want to know what you would do. Therefore, I find it supportive to say something like, "I'm happy to share what I would do, but first let's look at some things that might work for you."

Suppose your client says rhetorically, "Hmm, I wonder what would work best?" It's worthwhile to turn rhetorical questions back to them: "What do you think would work best?" They are often unbelievably powerful questions. And I discovered early on, clients more often than not have an answer.

WHEN YOU'RE STUCK AND HAVE NO IDEA WHAT TO ASK

It can easily happen to any coach at any time during a conversation that it isn't clear what to ask or where to go next. I often hear coaches struggle to come up with a question because they feel they're *supposed* to keep the conversation going. The easiest and simplest solution — *ask the client!* It is appropriate to remind your client what's been discussed and then ask, "What would be most helpful at this point?" They usually have something in mind that would help them gain more clarity.

That said, I've heard coaches ask clients, "What question do you want me to ask?" It is definitely *not* your client's role to figure out your job. If you have doubts as to how to proceed, ask your client, "What would be most helpful at this point?" You're simply asking for a direction that they believe will be helpful. On the rare occasion they can't answer, simply remind them of all that's been discussed up to that point and reconfirm what they are hoping for in the conversation. Now you have an easy way to handle not knowing what to ask at times in the conversation.

Coaches face a myriad of challenges with clients and their situations. Some of them are more complex and others repeat. As long as you know about several that could arise, you can be prepared to address them. And, there is nothing wrong with saying to a client who asks for something unusual, "I'll have to think about it and get back to you."

QUESTIONS FOR REFLECTION

- What opportunities might you have missed because you agreed with or shared a belief with your client? What will be different going forward when you notice you are agreeing with your client?
- What comes to mind when you consider dipping into feelings and yet staying out of therapy?
- What will you do differently when your client asks you a question or when you don't know what to ask?

CHAPTER 15

COMMUNICATION STYLES AND TYPES

Misunderstandings happen because we do not understand that different people have different styles of communication.
— Tony Alessandra

Assess your client's way of communicating to help tailor your approach to suit their needs. Because each individual has different desires, needs, and values, be prepared not to "cookie-cutter" your coaching.

Clients' styles are *behaviors or patterns of communication* that clients exemplify in coaching conversations and potentially elsewhere. The styles range from two extremes on the spectrum with corporate and restorative on each end with several in between. As a distinction, themes identify underlying thinking patterns and beliefs that keep clients stuck.

Following the descriptions of the styles of communicators is a section about the two broad types of people who come to us: "Thinkers" and "Feelers" — and those in between.

Corporate (not necessarily in a corporation)

This type of client probably doesn't have people with whom they can talk freely because they're either at the top of their company (the CEO) or hold a position of authority that they don't wish to compromise. Coaching provides an opportunity, so they unload and talk for a lot of the session. They move at a fast pace, know what they want, and have a clear agenda. They don't leave much room for you, so your questions or observations can make a big difference.

Restorative

The other extreme is the client who often wavers between needing therapy and coaching, and perhaps could use both. They might still be in therapy, or have just completed therapy, and are ready to start making more progress. It could be somebody who is simply fragile and doesn't necessarily need therapy but they're not a textbook coaching client either. They're on that edge. With restorative clients, you have to go *very* slowly and take tiny baby steps to avoid overwhelming them. A great deal of patience is required.

Full agenda

This client comes to sessions with a full agenda and selects the most important item to begin the session. They want to get right to work and reap the most benefit possible from each session. They will be frustrated with a slow pace or off-topic conversation.

No agenda

This client lacks a clear idea of what they want to work on at the beginning of the session. They just don't have a "story of the week." You can look at their overall patterns, as well as what they initially wanted from coaching, and then ask questions to help them uncover a pressing challenge. An option might be starting with their thoughts about their progress to date and recognizing what still needs addressing.

Unfocused

This client is all over the map. They bring up a lot but can't hone in on one thing they want to work on. One approach is to help them prioritize and figure out what is their most urgent item or find out how all their seemingly disparate items might be related.

Resistant

A resistant client consistently dodges questions and is unwilling to look inside. It's your role to "call them out" and find out what their resistance is really all about and/or what they might be avoiding. They might not be ready to make any changes even though they thought they were. In that case, you can discuss postponing coaching. Their resistance can also be an unwillingness to admit something because it's embarrassing or seems unimportant.

Lacks follow-through

No matter how excited this type of client seems about changing, they don't follow through. This can be because they've identified the wrong goal for themselves or there's something underneath that's in the way. A question that often works well is "What would it mean for you if this was finished?" That helps determine what the underlying fear might be. A classic example is when a client claims they want to develop a website, but it doesn't materialize. When you ask, "What would it mean if your website was up and running?" the typical answer is "Then people would see it" or "Then people would judge it."

Pleaser

This client believes they need to impress you and doesn't truly look within or go deep when exploring their challenges. It's as if they're trying to check off boxes. While it may feel good as a coach that your client is in such total compliance, it's not realistic. If they're acting this way during coaching, they're likely doing so elsewhere, so it's your role to find out what's behind this behavior.

Defiant

A defiant client uses an aggressive communication style even when trying to be productive. It could be that they were raised to communicate that way, or they live in a situation in which defiance and toughness are valued. Determine how this behavior impacts you. If it feels unpleasant, address it and help your client recognize that their defiance could impact others negatively as well. It's helpful to start with yourself: "When you speak in that tone, I feel as though I've done something wrong. What do you suppose it might mean for others?"

"I don't know — yet "

Your client might honestly not know how to answer a question about something outside of themselves. However, if your question is truly about them as a person, they probably do have an answer. If you sense that they're withholding an answer to a question, explore what's going on. They might feel ashamed or afraid to say it out loud. A helpful question is, "What would help you to know?" (versus the typical "What if you did know?") because the client almost always knows the answer.

Storyteller

Your client might enjoy telling stories and giving more examples and detail than is needed. It's never okay to interrupt the initial client story; however, when they're "recycling" information or repeating the same thing in different words, it's acceptable to intervene and point that out. They might be avoiding the real issue or it's just their style. Either way, it's an opportunity to point out how difficult it is to stay focused with so much detail. Alternatively, when you hear something relevant or an important word or phrase repeated, it's likely a good time to intervene and question it.

There are some important guidelines if you choose to intervene. First, start with their name because it immediately gets their attention: "John, I'm noticing the word *difficult* come up often. What made it so difficult for you?" Be sure to provide an explanation (context) for why you are interjecting: "John, I heard something important in what you just said, and I wonder what...."

Tight-lipped

When it's challenging to get information from your client, they might be feeling unsafe or avoiding something. First, work on establishing a greater degree of trust and intimacy. One way is to reflect what you've heard so they feel understood. If that doesn't help, remind them of the reason they came to you for coaching, and ask them if, in fact, they really want to make a change and move forward. Remember you are seeking data. If your client doesn't want to talk much, it's not about you. It's a clue that something is off, either in your relationship or inside of them.

Jargon-lover

This client uses a certain "lingo" to make them appear more intelligent or successful. Since speaking in jargon isn't natural, it might be helpful to point out and discover the reasons for its use.

Know-it-all

The know-it-all client consistently challenges, defends, and explains why something can't work. They consider their method or idea to be the best. It helps to point out how this often excludes other people and doesn't allow for any exchange. It can also be an opportunity to share how it makes you feel when they believe they already know everything.

Clients can fall into one or more of these communication styles. Being aware of them helps you approach your client in an impactful manner and probe about behaviors or styles that could be problematic for them.

THINKERS AND FEELERS

An intellectual, "thinking" client might not understand or recognize their feelings easily. For them it's all about the facts and their thoughts. Whereas if your client is very in touch with their feelings, they might need prompting to explore facts and logic. Interestingly, you will likely encounter a rather equal number of "thinkers" and "feelers."

You will likely recognize the type by listening for the word *think* or *feel* early on.

- Thinkers say things like "I thought it over," "I thought she would change," and "I think this would be...."
- Feelers say things like, "I felt so embarrassed," "He didn't even consider how I felt," "I was so worried I couldn't sleep," and, "I can feel it in my chest."

Once you've decided whether your new client is primarily a thinker or a feeler, tailor your questions accordingly.

Thinkers respond best to "backdoor" questions that don't address feelings head on, such as:

- What did you think when you heard that?
- What would it look like if that happened?
- What was happening for you during the meeting?
- What was going on for you when you witnessed that?

Feelers are most comfortable with questions like:

- What were you feeling when that happened?
- What emotions come up for you during these types of situations?
- What, if anything, has changed about your feelings regarding this?
- What's the strongest emotion you are experiencing now?

Don't ask a thinking person this standard coaching question: "Where do you feel this in your body?" I'm a thinker, and when someone asks me that question, I get embarrassed because I honestly don't know the answer. I typically make something up. Your thinking clients may have the same experience. On the other hand, this can be a wonderful question for a feeling person.

Not every question works across the board.

Usually it's easier to ask a feeling person questions because they more readily answer both thinking and feeling questions. It can be more difficult to come up with backdoor questions for thinking people to get to their feelings.

As a thinker I've learned to identify my feelings in the moment, and I have to keep practicing doing so. I initially studied a printed sheet showing all our different facial expressions (like emojis). When something didn't seem to click or work as I had hoped, I grabbed the sheet to identify what I was feeling. I'm sharing this so that if you're a feeler you can understand just how hard it can be for thinkers to answer a direct question about feelings.

No client is perfect. They're coming to you for help in understanding themselves more fully. By exploring their style together, your client will learn more about their patterns and be able to decide whether or not they wish to make any changes. This is especially important if their style is not supporting what they want.

QUESTIONS FOR REFLECTION

- What are some challenges you have experienced or foresee with a particular style of client?
- What might be some new ways to address a client who is a storyteller?
- What are some ways to address your client when you don't have the same communication style? If you're a thinker, what will help you address a feeler? If you're a feeler, what will help you address a thinker?

PART VI: MOVING FORWARD

CHAPTER 16

A DIFFERENT OPTION FOR INITIAL CONVERSATIONS WITH PROSPECTIVE CLIENTS

I've learned that people will forget what you said, people will forget what you did, but people will never forget how you made them feel.
— Maya Angelou

Having looked at an entire coaching conversation, client types and communication styles, advanced techniques, and coaching challenges, it's time to consider a different approach when first speaking with a client.

There are many different approaches to the start of a relationship with a prospective client. Some coaches offer a complimentary consultation, others a complimentary coaching session, others no more than a very brief conversation, and some charge for a two-hour discovery session. You can decide what works best for you.

In my experience, a great deal of what you need to know is revealed in the first conversation. It's an opportunity not only for the prospective client, but also for you, to ascertain if this is someone with whom you'd like to be in a coaching relationship.

Building rapport and discussing logistics, rather than solving a problem, is the purpose of the first conversation. It doesn't have to be longer than thirty minutes. There are two primary reasons for not getting into a full coaching conversation during an initial session:

1. Your client might think that their problem is solved and there's no need to continue.

2. Your client might decide that their problems are too big and/or will take too much work to resolve.

To take a lot of pressure off, all that's really needed on your part is good reflection, so your client feels truly heard, and a few questions either for clarity or to better understand them. You'll hopefully leave them with something to think about if and when you speak again.

QUESTIONS TO PREPARE YOUR CLIENT FOR THEIR FIRST SESSION

While some people look for a coach with specifics in mind, others don't really know what kind of coach they want or need. Sending a prospective client a few questions before your first meeting can be helpful. Be sure to tell them that answering them before their first session is *optional*. I send out the questions below and mention that their answers might help structure our first conversation. Some people ignore them, some come prepared with detailed answers, and others are somewhere in between.

1. What are your three biggest challenges? OR What is your main reason for wanting coaching?

2. What would your life look like if everything was resolved? [The ideal]

3. What would your life look like if nothing changed? [The present situation]

4. What's preventing you from solving your challenges on your own? [Why they need you]

SETTING THE STAGE

While some new coaches have a hard time believing that a prospective client can be more nervous than they are, it's possible because their client is about to reveal information to a stranger that they may never have shared before. Since both of you might be nervous, set the stage to make your first conversation more comfortable.

Both you and your client might have some trepidation or concerns as to how the conversation will unfold and about pricing, rapport, etc. I developed the introduction below to calm me down. Fortunately, it also works really well for the client, and immediately puts them at ease. It addresses the ground rules while building trust and rapport.

After the initial greetings and minimal small talk, I mention that coaching is a partnership, and it's not about my giving advice. Rather, I tell them that together we will find what works best for them. I let them know that it will be entirely their agenda and what they're willing to share. Here's my introduction to Melissa:

* * *

Melissa, I'm going to explain how we will spend our time. I will be listening to you share what's going on for you and what you hope to gain from coaching. I will be asking you questions. Some of them might be for me to get clarity, and some of them might actually be thought-provoking.

And because of that, there may be times in our conversation when we'll have some silence. [Because we're on the phone and can't see each other] whenever there's silence, I'm going to wait for you to speak first. That way, in case you're thinking or writing something, I won't be interrupting your thoughts.

Because I'll be asking you so many questions and hearing all about you, I think it's only fair that you're able to ask me questions. So, if you have questions and things you really want to know about me that you think would be relevant and helpful, then of course feel free to do so.

Sometimes I write things down. Sometimes I don't. I just want you to know what's happening on my end. When

251

we get to the end of our conversation, I'm going to ask you what you thought about it, and then we'll take about ten minutes or so to discuss how coaching works, how much it costs, how much time is involved, and all those logistical pieces. [*Announcing that the pricing discussion comes at the end relieves both the client's and coach's anxiety regarding that discussion.*]

Before we begin, and before you tell me what's going on, let me know if you have any questions. [*Let the client answer.*]

Now go ahead, Melissa, and as best as you can, let me know me what's going on for you. [*Or any open invitation to begin the conversation.*]

It's not necessary to have a long, involved conversation to pick up on the essentials about the person. If your client is new to coaching, they have no idea what to expect. Asking them questions about how they want things to be handled or addressed at this point seems premature. Many of the qualities and characteristics of a person show up in the first conversation, providing information about their preferences without having to ask. You might not realize the relevance of this data right then, but it can be highly informative and stored in your "databank."

NOTICING THEMES

During the initial session, a client often mentions a few issues they're having, thinking they're totally unrelated. You can usually find a common thread that you can store in your mental databank. This allows you to share with your client a potential direction or plan for the coaching engagement.

Rosalie came to her initial coaching conversation with three issues:

- My husband is always putting me down.

- My closest friend is always late and it's really annoying.
- My mother is constantly interfering in my relationship with my daughter.

Although the three situations seem to be totally unrelated to Rosalie, the coach noticed that all three situations relate to setting boundaries. By pointing out this common theme, he enabled her to gain a deeper awareness and, consequently, they created a bond that inspired her to continue with coaching.

Instead of asking which one of the three is most important as a starting place, recognize a potential common thread. This immediately demonstrates that you have a deeper understanding as well as already creating awareness.

DETERMINING IF YOU'RE A GOOD MATCH

Remember that an initial session is for you and your prospective client to determine whether or not you're a good match. With tongue in cheek, I often tell new coaches without a coaching niche to, "Take anyone who's breathing." And early on this can expose you to many types of people and help you narrow down the types of clients you prefer. One of the most important things for you to discern is whether or not you believe the person is coachable; that is, do they seem open and willing to do what it takes to resolve their challenges.

Here are some things to look for in the first conversation to determine whether or not you will work well together:

- Is the client trauma-based and in need of therapy?
- Is the client too focused on wanting to go back into history versus wanting to move forward?
- Is the client expecting advice and answers from you?
- Is the client able to commit to the process and able to pay?

The first conversation is also an opportunity to determine your compatibility with the prospective client. Each coach is responsible for determining who are their best clients. No one can serve everyone. Consider these topics:

- You might not want to work with someone whose focus is of little interest to you.
- Some people talk so much that they leave little space for the coach, while others are extremely slow and process out loud. One or the other might be irritating or annoying to you.
- Some people are results-oriented and agenda-driven and it may not jive with your values.
- Some people need more hand-holding and can only move in small, incremental steps. For some this is frustrating.
- A prospective client might have challenges that clash with your value system, such as they are having an affair while married. If their situation is unpleasant for you, you can pass on such a client.
- You might not want to work with someone who doesn't inspire trust and an easy rapport.
- Some people expect answers and solutions rather than exploration and discovery. They might not be willing to do the necessary work.
- A person might evoke your bias and judgment, so it's probably better for both of you not to work together because objectivity may be compromised.

You are *not* going to want to coach every prospective client who comes to you. It's your right to proceed with only those who are good matches for you.

CLOSING THE INITIAL SESSION

After discussing the logistics and listening to your client's assessment of the initial conversation, it's up to you to let them know if moving forward is favorable or if you prefer not to coach them.

If you align with the person and want to move forward, let them know! Be explicit as to why you think you can be helpful, and mention something about them that appeals to you, such as their willingness to be open. If, on the other hand, you don't feel you're compatible, simply say something like, "I don't believe I'm the best coach for your situation. I believe there are others who would be better suited." This doesn't offend them or make them wrong in any way. And if you know a coach who would be better suited, by all means recommend that person.

When you use this format for your initial sessions, you'll gather important data about your prospective client, provide them with the experience of talking with you and feeling heard, and cover the logistics of coaching in an easy and professional manner — all without creating a feeling of pressure. Instead, you'll be inviting them to collaborate with you in a coaching relationship if you feel interested in working with them. You'll begin your partnership right from the start, and you'll set the stage for an effective and profound coaching relationship.

QUESTIONS FOR REFLECTION

- What do you like (or not like) about your current process for initial client conversations?
- What, if any, inspiration do you have for making some changes in your current process?
- What has been your experience when you decided to go ahead with someone when your intuition told you it wasn't a good match?

CHAPTER 17

A SAMPLE OF A LASER-FOCUSED COACHING SESSION

As we know, there are many different pathways to get to the same results. Because we are working with people who are unique in their own way, there is no right way since everything unfolds as it does.

That said, I'm including this particular coaching conversation in its entirety (thirty minutes) along with my thinking process, because it demonstrates all of the elements of Laser-Focused Coaching and emphasizes that we don't need any details. Because Becky is a coach, we agreed ahead of time that we would review the coaching from her perspective when we completed. Her feedback follows the full conversation.

Coach: In our time today, Becky, what is it that we can look at, focus on, that's going to be really of importance to you?

Becky: Okay, well, in my coaching, I really would like to narrow down a niche, some place I can focus on. I feel like I really need a focal point to move forward in my practice and in my business to get that started. So, I have got a couple of directions that keep pulling me in a couple of different, like very different directions. And I feel like I need to figure out where I need to be going.

[Since she stated what she is looking for rather clearly, the conversation could begin to move forward.]

Coach: Your dilemma about finding a direction is certainly understandable. What is it about having these different directions that's making this tricky for you?

[After normalizing her feelings, I wondered, "What is making this a problem for her?" I also picked up on the ambivalence theme. If I make one decision over the other, I will lose something. This helped me keep the big picture in mind while putting these thoughts in my "databank."]

Becky: I think because they're so different. I feel like they're almost kind of not opposite, but very different — going in a very different direction. They are really two, way different things. So, I get pulled both ways. So, I feel like I need to narrow that down and have some clarity around what it is I need to be focusing on. Maybe it's just for the moment, maybe it's just for now, but to try to get some clarity around that.

Coach: And what is important to you about getting that clarity?

[Deepening the agreement by finding out what the relevance is for her of getting clarity.]

Becky: I think it's stopping me from moving forward. I think this is kind of a big obstacle for me to move forward and to start a business and start something significant in a direction because I'm wavering.

Coach: It sounds like in your mind, once you get clear on this direction, or a specific niche, then you can move forward. What would moving forward look like?

[I reflected what I heard and went right to a question. I wanted to know what her vision was while deepening the agreement.]

Becky: Moving forward with the kind of solidifying a business and then doing all the… everything is based on that, from what I'm getting, and learning and understanding. It's all kind of based around one idea, and if it's, these are two different ideas. It's one, if I get one, then I focus on one and everything I need to know, write, and to, let's say, thinking about my client avatar, and who I want to be coaching and who I want to be talking to — it all becomes clear.

Coach: And the way it's sounding, it's as if there's an either/or going on. And I wonder what if it wasn't an either/or, what would that mean for you?
[I named the Either/Or theme and then removed the obstacle.]

Becky: That would make it much easier if I could do everything, right? But I think that there, there's two such different ideas and directions that, they don't really combine with each other. Okay. So, if I, and I think I've been trying to kind of figure out where's the middle in all of this, but I don't think there really is.

Coach: Yeah, that almost sounds like jack of all trades, master of none....

Becky: Yeah, and I think I want to avoid that. I want to avoid just coaching everybody, and I've done that. I've been there, done that, and I don't like it.

So, you know, coaching anybody and everybody that is willing. So I have narrowed... let's say I've raised prices, so I've narrowed all these people that just really want somebody to talk to. I've gotten those people out which leaves very few clients. However, I want to be able to speak to a specific group and narrow that down.

Coach: It sounds like, I want to say almost choosing one over the other, at least as a starting point....

Becky: Right.

Coach: Based on that, you said you've narrowed down to just a few people. And what has happened in relation to the two ideas that are seemingly opposed when you look at the people that you've narrowed down?
[I needed clarity on what she was saying, because it wasn't totally clear to me.]

Becky: You know what, that's a very good question. Actually, the people that I've narrowed down to the ones that I did great prices, it took away a lot of the people of one of those groups.

Coach: So, what does that say to you?

[It seems as though she deepened her awareness from the simple question. I needed to find out if that was the case and what it meant for her.]

Becky: Yeah, actually… when you asked me that, I was like, "Oh, you're right." Yes, that maybe this group of people really does need somebody that's kind of more than a coach, really hold their hand and be a friend.

Coach: So, it's the rent-a-friend versus that coach…
[While reflecting, she jumped in.]

Becky: That, or not willing to pay or not… they're not able to pay for the coaching.

Coach: When you think about those people that have been, I want to say, almost eliminated, what comes up for you in terms of regrets, and /or that's fine?
[I needed to get clarity on how she felt about that group of people and possibly letting them go. The following questions were dependent on her answer.]

Becky: There, I think there's both of that's fine, because I wasn't getting any compensation or significant compensation. I mean, if I'm getting paid less than a dog walker, I think that's bad.

So, the compensation wasn't there. However, I empathize with these people so much because I know what their situation is because I guess I've been there. I know what they're going through. I know the process, and I empathize with them so much—because it's difficult what they're dealing with.

Coach: And what is it about this other group other than they can pay, what is it about that group that, I want to say excites you, or if you had to let go would be difficult?
[Since I got a clue about one group, I now needed data and clarity about the other group before moving the conversation forward.]

Becky: Well, it does excite me because it's exciting to watch them grow. Like small business owners. I mean, that's exciting for me. I do also have a background in business, and I'm getting my master's in organizational behavior and leadership. These are in fields that I'm very interested in also. And it is exciting to watch them just take off. So, that gives me a lot of positive energy. It just does, and it's exciting.

Coach: What I'm getting then is, the one group is, I'm going to say in quotes "familiar" in terms of identifying, and the other one, it sounds like it really energizes you. So, if you had to let go of one, what would that mean?
[I reflected what it sounded like to me and then found out what's really true but not yet asking for a choice!]

Becky: What would it mean… [PAUSE] I think if I let go, I feel like I do have to let go of one because it's that they're too different, I guess, right?

My personal experiences have led me through the one group that when I raise prices, they all fell off. So, what would it mean to me, if I would let those go? I don't know, maybe, my immediate feeling that I got was that was a little bit of relief which is surprising to me also. It's a lot. It's a very emotional state to be in. It's very emotional for me to be there. And so, it makes me a little bit sad, but I think my immediate reaction was, kind of relief, thinking about letting that go.
[Notice her out loud processing and further awareness. Because of her initial pause, I left total silence to let her keep going.]

Coach: Hmm. Let's suppose that you are choosing the one that is much more lucrative and energizes you.

Becky: Mm-hmm.

Coach: And for now, you let go of the one where you feel very passionate about helping these people, and they really do need the coaching, but they're also not able to really compensate you financially in a way that makes sense. What does that look like for you?
[I preliminarily "painted the picture" to see where she is because it "seems" as though she has somewhat made a choice.]

Becky: So, let that go?

261

Coach: Mm-hmm.

Becky: So, my feeling is, am I letting something go that maybe I was supposed to? Somewhere I went through this journey, this is where I'm supposed to be kind of thing. So, is this a path that I'm not choosing because it's not as easy, it's not as lucrative, or it's not as easy, I'd say? Emotionally easy, also. So, am I choosing? Am I copping out? You know, it would be challenging. It's going to be, I mean, it is kind of a challenging subject, and I have a lot of knowledge in it.

And so, I do have the background and the knowledge, and kind of "I've been there, done that" kind of thing. So, I don't, I feel like, is this a cop out? Am I just taking the easy way out?

I'm not living up to the potential of what I'm supposed to use. Why? Why am I finding myself here at this right now, kind of idea? And do I need to make this step into that area where I would certainly have an impact and be really useful to people, I think? But it's a harder way.

Coach: You're asking the question, am I copping out? What do you think?

[I turned her question right back to her before continuing beyond that.]

Becky: I think, I don't know. I really thought about it. And I honestly don't know if I'm being super, super honest with myself. I feel like maybe, yes, I am copping out, go the easy way and I do like the program, right? Follow the steps and do what I'm kind of supposed to do. Also, in a way I was building this business, this is my problem. So, in my going to, yeah, it's difficult. I think I am, in a way, copping out because I don't want to go there every day. I don't want to have conversations that surround this every day; it was painful. I think it might be a little bit of a cop out.

Coach: It's interesting that you use the word *painful.* So it seems like it would be a struggle; it would be painful. I'm wondering if this could be more about making a sensible choice rather than copping

out. What do you think? *[LONG SILENCE]*
[I picked up on her emotion, shared my thoughts, and questioned her. This reflection and question led Becky to discovering what was really behind her indecision.]

Becky: I'm sorry, I'm thinking. I think it's a logical choice to kind of choose the more structured and less emotional side of this coaching. So, I think that's more logical. And the other painful way, I mean, I can see it to be painful, and would it be more rewarding? Maybe.

Would it be more rewarding in the long run? It's possible, too. *[SILENCE]* So, I have thought about this for a long time. I just, I don't like, I don't know, I guess… *[SILENCE]* yeah, I feel like it's a teeter totter. I mean, I'll think about it for a while with all the yes and no, and then yes, and I go back and forth. And so, why is that? Why am I doing that to myself? *[SILENCE]*

The first thing that popped in my mind when I said that, "Why am I doing this to myself?" it's like, well, if you don't make a choice, then you don't have to move forward.
[Notice how much silence I allowed for her to keep processing out loud. And that led to her aha! realization that was at the crux of the problem.]

Coach: Yeah, feels safer in a phony way; what do you think?
[She just had a major awareness, so not a big question or trying to move forward. It was an opportunity to let her keep processing — which she does.]

Becky: Yeah. Well, that's exactly what pops into my mind and that let's say, would make sense for me, too. If I don't, if I don't make a choice and I don't have to, then I don't have to go through the other steps. And I will be stuck, anyway, like I've always wanted to which is the bigger cop out than either one of them.
[Even deeper awareness emerged for her.]

Coach: That sounds true. What is going to help you to make this decision?
[Now it was time to move the conversation forward. I'm still not totally sure what she is choosing.]

Becky: Ummm. I don't think either one is wrong. I do think that either one is… it's not like I'm getting a tattoo. So, it's not permanent.

Coach: Right.

Becky: It's not something that I need to be able to be a little bit more flexible. Focus on one. I think, to choose one, at least for now, and allow myself to move forward in that. And I think that the realization that I had was that this back and forth in my head was probably a kind of self-defence mechanism.

Coach: Yes.

Becky: So, I don't make that step. So, *[pause]* so just even the realization that that's what's going on in my head is huge. *[SILENCE]*

So, what do I need to move forward to make a choice? I think I need to focus on one. I don't have to maybe even choose one or the other. I can focus on one for now.

And I'm sure that people, it happens organically, anyway. The people that want my help in this other aspect come to me naturally. It happens. I can't even explain how that happened. It's the power of attraction.

[She organically created her own action and plan.]

Coach: Mm-hmm. It is, yes.

Becky: And it doesn't stop me from helping them either.

Coach: That's right. What I'm taking from all this is that the idea of being so stuck is actually worse than at least starting with a focus on one versus the other, and that neither one will eliminate the other. Where are things, then, in our conversation at this point, considering where we started, and you were totally undecided?

[I interpreted what she shared and then "looped" to see just how much she still needs and where things are with her. I needed to know for sure if she was ready to close down.]

Becky: Well, I think, I don't have to choose one or the other. Well, I mean, I have to focus on one, but I don't have to choose. I have to focus on one and put energy behind one, one that is probably going to be lucrative, something that's going to be able to have an income, and then be open to help. But to have a focal point that I need to move forward and setting up a business and moving forward and getting that organized, I feel like, it's so logical, that's logical.

And I don't have to eliminate one, the one that where kind of that passion is, right? The passion, which is the one that takes spending a lot of emotional energy... it's a lot of emotion. It's a lot of what I don't maybe necessarily even want right now.

Coach: At this point, what are you learning about yourself in all this?
[I continued to deepen and broaden her awareness.]

Becky: Learning that the obstacle that I thought was obvious is, probably, just a mechanism for holding me back, and holding me in the same pattern, this kind of landing pattern like, okay, make a choice, but the choice was really not that it's just the choice of moving forward. So, yeah, that surprised me, yeah.

Coach: And I just wonder if there's any place else in your life where this teeter-tottering might play a role that might be holding you back from something?
[Notice how I used her vocabulary and the bonus question because it seemed logical in this case (ambivalence).]

Becky: [SILENCE] Mmm. I'm not sure. Like, in my personal life, or another aspect?

Coach: Mm-hmm.

Becky: I think that what's popping up for me is probably learning. I'm a new coach. And so, I feel like I just need to learn as much as possible and it's fascinating, number one, but it also limits my time in physically coaching, too. So, that could be another aspect where I'm using, learning, and exploring, and studying to not put time and effort into building a business.

Coach: What, if anything, is coming up just even realizing that? *[Again, deepening her awareness and allowing her time to reflect on what she said.]*

Becky: I think, I don't think that I was aware of this before. So, I think it hasn't been something that I've been aware of, but how significant it is in holding me back, I guess. But I do feel like I really want to get good at the skills, and I really want to be able to be effective in what I do. And then there's a little bit of confidence-building there, too, and I am....

I'm doing it on purpose as well to be able to have that confidence. And so, I think it's two-fold, but the one, the stuff's that's really holding me back, though, was the choice of where am I going to go because I do get pulled and I do get asked, pulled in certain directions a lot. And so, it's that I don't think that they're mutually exclusive. And I do think it's... do you think there's physical cues for me not to move forward — in one of them?

Coach: What do you think about physical cues not to move forward? *[Again, I turned her question right back to her.]*

Becky: No, not really. I don't think so.

Coach: Now that you've reached this point, what kind of support, perhaps somebody or something that could help you as you now begin to settle in on at least a starting place? *[NOW, it was time to ask about support and resources for her forward movement.]*

Becky: Actually, I do have, I have another coach set up to really help to find the niche more specifically. And so, I do have people and an organization that I'm working with to really dive into it because I know this is a problem, it has been a problem.

So, I'm involved in a group that's actively doing that. I think that's going to help really, and just to get this clear in my head was a huge obstacle. So, now that I have that kind of clarity, I'm going to... I can run with it and push it forward.

Coach: That sounds convincing. You certainly have come a long way in this conversation from indecision to clarity. I heard a lot of processing and great insights that you discovered. Is there anything else then that you need in this conversation, or are we in a place to stop?

[It was important to reflect how she sounded (as opposed to tentative). I then championed her and checked with her if she was okay to end. It felt like it to me but I couldn't make that decision.]

Becky: I got exactly what I needed. That's the thing: I'm good.

Coach: You're okay to stop?

Becky: Uh-huh.

Coach: Okay, then let's stop here.

> NOTE: I never needed to know
> what the niches were.
> Becky already knew what they were —
> to ask would have been my "nosey" curiosity.

REVIEW AND FEEDBACK FROM BECKY

Coach: Let's take a moment then. From your perspective, what were some of the things that were really helpful or anything that you noticed from the coaching? I know you were truly the client, so it's hard to critique it from the other end. But maybe, perhaps, anything you can say about it?

Becky: Right off the bat I noticed that you didn't let me talk about the problem which is a mistake I normally make with my clients. You had no idea what the two choices were! And that was really effective, especially for me because I usually think there is a certain way I'm supposed to do things. I think that was really, really effective because I didn't get a chance to talk about that. My first thought was, "Oh, she's never going to ask me what my two choices are." And you didn't.

267

And what else did I notice? That you allowed me to flip-flop back and forth, because I did a lot of that. You allowed that to happen several times until I landed on something.

But I think, and I don't remember the exact question that you asked where I thought, "Oh, maybe this is a little bit deeper." And that was a very effective question. *["It's interesting that you use the word painful. So it seems like it would be a struggle; it would be painful. I'm wondering if this could be more about making a sensible choice rather than copping out. What do you think?"]* That question allowed me to get to what's holding me back from making the decision.

I also noticed how much silence you left quite a few times. It was really hard for me to get in there and figure out, "What is going on?" That silence was powerful because it allowed me to really dig in — really dig in. That's why I'm talking to you. I want you to give me the answer. It would be so easy.

QUESTION FOR REFLECTION

- What do you notice from this coaching conversation, and everything you've read, that will be helpful as you move forward in your coaching?

A FINAL WORD

Now that you've come to the end of *Laser-Focused Coaching*, I hope you feel stronger, wiser, and more confident in your ability to help your clients change their lives. I also hope your brain is buzzing with ideas about all the ways you can implement the new skills you've discovered.

The best way to master the concepts and tools in this book is to use them. Give yourself some time to achieve mastery. Much of what you read may be brand new, review, or extremely different from your current coaching approach. If you're familiar with this approach, perhaps there were some additional ideas that you'll try out and experiment with.

As with learning any new approach, it might be daunting to try to implement everything at once. My recommendation is to first choose principles and concepts that seem easy to try out, or if you are an experienced coach, choose ideas that could have a major impact on your coaching. Since everyone's style is so different, pick and choose what works best for you, while remembering that enhancing your listening and communication skills is the bedrock of all masterful coaching.

Above all, remember the distinction between transactional and Laser-Focused Coaching. I invite you to go deep with your clients and to help them explore their beliefs, habits, and perceptions so they can choose new views that enrich every aspect of their lives. Now that you have some new insights and ideas, you'll be able to provide transformational coaching in an effective manner so that your clients see progress after each session beyond an action or temporary strategy that solves their immediate situation.

When you employ deep, transformational coaching, you will be coaching at a more masterful level. The process is simple, but not easy. You'll need time, practice, and commitment to consistently coach in this more profound way. Your clients will appreciate the depth of change, and eventually learn tools and principles they can use when they complete the coaching engagement. You'll help your clients transform their lives permanently and for the better. I can't think of anything more powerful and compelling than that.

ABOUT THE AUTHOR

As a Master Certified Coach (MCC), Marion Franklin is sought after for her Laser-Focused approach and direct communication. Her work includes developing and teaching her unique program, *Laser Coach Your Way to Sustainable Success – Intensive,* which emphasizes masterful coaching skills. She published the audiobook *Life's Little Lessons: Improve Your Life One Lesson at a Time*, facilitates ongoing "Coach with Confidence" mentor groups, and provides individual mentoring and supervising.

To date, everyone Marion has taught and mentored for Associate Certified Coach (ACC), Professional Certified Coach (PCC), or Master Certified Coach (MCC) has passed (using the principles from this book). She serves as a supervisory coach and examiner for developing coaches in an executive coaching program, has been interviewed on TV for her coaching expertise, coached executives at various corporations, presented at numerous coaching conferences and events, and has been cited in *The Journal News* and *The Wall Street Journal.*

Marion holds master's degrees in business and education. Prior to coaching, she co-founded a healthcare publishing company and taught high school business education. Aside from coach training and mentoring, she finds it critical to maintain individual coaching clients. Through them she is richly rewarded as they move toward and achieve their sustainable visions. In her spare time, Marion takes drawing classes and plays bridge and she resides in Tarrytown, New York.

http://www.lifecoachinggroup.com

To receive **The Top 10 Myths Coaches Believe**, go here: http://www.lifecoachinggroup.com/readergift

271

Her services include:
Coach Training – Laser Coach Your Way to Sustainable Success
Individual and Group Mentoring
Supervision
Individual Coaching

AudioBook: *Life's Little Lessons: Improve Your Life One Lesson at a Time*
Subscribe and sample: lifecoachinggroup.com
To view the 99 topics: lifecoachinggroup.com/audiobook.php

Website: lifecoachinggroup.com
E-mail: marion@lifecoachinggroup.com

ACKNOWLEDGMENTS

There are so many caring and supportive people who have contributed to this book; to my knowledge, my coaching, and my mentoring skills; and to my personal growth. Without you, this book would not have been written. As they say on the Academy Awards: If I've left anyone out, I sincerely apologize.

First and foremost, Tony A. Kirkland. Not only did Tony introduce me to coaching, and train and mentor me, his influence and his coaching changed my life exponentially and catapulted my coaching acumen. His genius is always with me.

I would never be where I am today if it weren't for the late Thomas J. Leonard. Thomas, one of the greatest inspirations and coaches of all time, taught me coaching nuances and skills that, to this day, impact my coaching and training. His responsiveness and generosity will forever be unrivalled.

Andrea J. Lee, the first person who believed in my work enough to allow me to teach and share my knowledge. To this day, I am grateful that Andrea trusted in my ability to teach coaching skills, as it led to the teaching and training that I continue to do today.

Cheryl Richardson, whom I met when her first book (of many) was released. It became my resource for workshops when I first started out. She has been a role model for Laser-Focused Coaching, and she inspired me to gain a deeper understanding of boundaries.

Every student and mentee over the past twenty-five years has contributed to my mission by taking their coaching skills to heart and then turning around and positively impacting thousands of clients around the world. Thanks for your steadfast trust, advocacy, and support.

All of my coaching clients I've been privileged to serve and learn from. Because of you I continue to hone my skills and learn more about life every day.

The undying devotion, support, trust, and love that I've received from Nikki Brown is immeasurable. Not only has she helped me on a daily basis with administrative tasks and allowed me to brainstorm whenever needed, her ongoing participation in my mentor group propelled her coaching beyond expectation, and that makes my heart soar.

Having known Lynne Klippel for over twenty years, she was my go-to person when I knew that this book had to be written. Her enthusiasm and ongoing support have kept me in tow.

Without David Franklin's guidance, tenacity, and aligned coaching knowledge, this book would not be what it is. His patience and commitment to masterful coaching has strongly influenced this book. His personal growth journey influences mine as well as my coaching.

Karen Leigh has been an ongoing inspiration with her insights, candidness, and modeling of personal growth. Her influence has furthered my learning about human behavior.

A huge thank you goes to my early readers. Tian Vickers for her editing prowess, steadfast encouragement, and advocacy; Heidi Connal for her loyal support, trust, and tolerance; Merci Miglino for her ongoing reassurance and contributions; Meghan Kuhn for her dependability and support; and Shelley Grice for her support and trust. Because of your thoughts, comments, and praise, this book has made it out into the world.

I want to acknowledge my gratitude and appreciation for Nathan Kreger. He has consistently pulled through and executed every request. His technical expertise, along with his coaching skill and ideas, has been invaluable.

Thanks to Nina Kaufman for believing in what I offer to the coaching world and encouraging me to write this book. Also, for all of the preliminary work leading to the birth of this book.

Thanks to John-Paul Beals for being my muse. Without you, the words never would have made it to paper.

Thanks to Kirsten Allen, who was my teaching assistant for several years. Her steadfastness and creative thinking and contributions made teaching more interesting and classes more dynamic.

Enormous appreciation for my masterful coach colleagues who provided unrivaled group coaching: Amy Armstrong, Angela DeSousa, Ellen Fulton, and Libby Graves.

I am so blessed to have such wonderful friends and supporters. Karen P., your undying belief in me and your encouragement is above and beyond. Carole, for being such an empathic and understanding listener. Kathy, for upgrading our conversations and for our special friendship. Judy, someone I can always count on and who remains level-headed and supportive. Valerie, for truly accepting me as I am and helping me see the light when necessary. Jane, for wanting me to succeed and organizing so many fun things to do together. Jackie P., thank you for your never-ending belief in me and my work. Susan L., for your wordsmithing. Mary, for your listening and understanding. And Vivian, my sister, for being with me through all of life's ups and downs.

INDEX

Locators in "**bold**" are diagrams; locators in "*italics*" are tables.

Made in the USA
Columbia, SC
16 May 2023

16778902R00161